Reflections on the Water

By the same author

Angling in Earnest
Successful Angling (*contributor*)
One for the Pot
Fishing for Tench
Guide to Ferreting
My Fishing Years

Reflections on the Water

THE BEST OF FRED J. TAYLOR

Compiled by Fred Rashbrook

Illustrated by Ted Andrews

BUCHAN & ENRIGHT, PUBLISHERS
LONDON

First published in 1982 by
Buchan & Enright, Publishers, Limited
21 Oakley Street, London SW3 5 NT

ISBN 0 907675 05 0

Printed in Great Britain by
Richard Clay (The Chaucer Press) Ltd
Bungay, Suffolk
Filmset in Monophoto Bembo by
Northumberland Press Ltd, Gateshead

Contents

Contents

Introduction

A lifelong follower of country pursuits, Fred J. Taylor brings to his writings on fishing and kindred topics a rich fund of experience and accumulated knowledge which is enlivened by his capacity for shrewd observation of the outdoor scene. And through it all, his warm friendliness and strong sense of humour are communicated to his readers in a way which has firmly established him as one of the most popular and widely read writers in his field.

His knowledge of angling is extensive and over the years he has made important contributions to the thinking which has influenced the development of modern fishing tackle and methods. In this, however, as with all his other sporting activities, Fred's prime concern has always been the simple pleasure to be derived from it by the participant. Once fishing ceases to be fun, it no longer rates with Fred as a desirable form of recreation.

This, perhaps more than any other aspect of his approach to the subject, provides the linking theme for the chapters of this book, which has been compiled from carefully selected samples of his contributions to various national newspapers and periodicals. Over a period of many years, Fred has written regularly for the *Standard*, the *Shooting Times and Country Magazine*, the *Sunday Telegraph*, *Angler's Mail*, *Angling Magazine*, and numerous other publications, and now this book will ensure that some of the best of this material will have the wider readership and longer life that it so richly deserves.

The subjects range widely, covering Fred's encounters with such species as roach, perch, carp, bream, eels, pike, trout and salmon, as well as American largemouth bass and bluegills, frogs, glow-worms—and possible ghosts. He recounts all these adventures in his own eminently readable style with many humorous sketches of incidents and characters—some rather eccentric—he has come across on the way.

He also contrives to instruct as well as entertain the reader, for there is a great deal of angling wisdom and know-how to be gleaned from his carefully observed descriptions of successes—and failures—experienced at the waterside.

Fred Rashbrook

Fred J. Taylor would like to express his gratitude to the Editors of *Angler's Mail* and the *Shooting Times and Country Magazine* for their confidence in him, and for giving their permission to reproduce in this book articles that originally appeared in their publications. I am also very grateful to Ted Andrews for his marvellous scraper-board illustrations.

Early Years

Are there any memories, I wonder, more vivid than childhood memories; and of them all, if you are a fisherman, are there any that stand out more than early fishing memories?

Sometimes I'm sure I can remember every single fishing trip I ever took in my childhood, and yet I cannot remember the first one, for it seems that I have always been fishing. I was brought up in an atmosphere of bamboo roach poles, hickory pike rods, wooden reels, silk lines and hooks to gut. The sweet smell of stewing wheat, toppings and bran mixed with bread in the great zinc bath, cans of live bait under the dripping top, lines drying on chair-backs before being stretched across the garden for the greasing ritual after each trip, lobworms in flat tobacco tins full of freshly gathered moss, linen bags of paste and dough bait—all these were part of our regular household scene. Dad, you see, was a fisherman, and because fishing in those days was different in so many respects from what it is today, the preparations for each coming weekend's fishing were always in evidence. They never stopped throughout the season.

When I was a small child we lived literally on the bank of the river and it was only necessary in those days to walk down to the bottom of the garden to begin fishing—but, alas, we moved before I grew old enough to wield a rod for myself.

I was never *taught* to fish. I was just allowed to go on some of the fishing trips and, when I was big enough, was given an outfit to use. I remember that outfit: two top joints of a roach pole, a fixed line, a shotted float and a hook. With it, naturally, I learned to catch roach; they were the first fish I ever caught, which is perhaps why they're still my favourite fish.

All that, however was under the guidance of an adult. I remember my excitement and trembling hands, and the difficulty I had rebaiting after each fish, and I shall always be grateful that I was allowed to start to learn about fishing that way. But I believe my real apprenticeship started after I was given a rod of my own and allowed to go fishing with the other kids. I'd graduated from 'bannies' (sticklebacks) to minnows and gudgeon on a garden cane by that time and now, at last, I had joined the lucky ones who could fish the lake and the canal.

We weren't all that bright as fishermen, really. We were too noisy, our tackle was crude and our techniques shocking. We figured that all the fish were lying out farther than we could reach and so we all tried to outcast each other. We developed a rig which we always referred to as 'light line and heavy tackle' for helping us to cast great distances. We used lines of about three pounds' breaking strain and huge floats cocked by a great string of shots, and we stripped yards of line off our reels at our feet so that it would run freely through the rod rings. Every so often one of us would make a super cast and the red-topped float would settle and cock many yards out in the middle of the lake.

More often than not we just *hoped* that the bait was still on; we dared not wind in to make sure because there was too much involved. Not that it mattered much, anyway. There was always a breeze to catch the big float and the greased floating line and drag it all back to the bank within a matter of minutes—that or the float was dragged under!

It's a wonder we ever caught any fish at all, but we did. Roach, rudd, perch and, occasionally, eels. And though we'd all been taught to return them at once, I fear that very few of them survived the rigours of being passed along the bank for inspection by a dozen grubby-handed juveniles.

We may have been lacking in technical knowledge and in angling skill, we were short on patience (which is perhaps no bad thing), we had no transport other than our beat-up bikes, but there was one commodity of which we had a super-abundance. We had time! And we did not waste it.

We knew how to get up in the mornings and, with a bottle of water, lemonade or cold tea and a great pile of sandwiches (which our harassed mothers were no doubt pleased to cut for us in the interests of peace and quiet), we would be installed at the water by dawn. If one of our number failed to turn up at the appointed hour we did not wait. We went without him. That was the rule in those days, and I think it is a pity that such a rule is not adhered to today. If we could do it on push-bikes it ought to be possible to arrive on time with today's modern transport.

Even today, some forty years later, those who fished with me in those early days, and still do occasionally today, know the rule. They would not wait for me should I be late, and they do not expect me to wait for them. That is how it ought to be and how it always will be with me. Many of my more recently made friends have been surprised and hurt when they have arrived at a meeting-place fifteen minutes late and found that I have gone on without them. They have been surprised despite the fact that I have warned them what would happen. I refuse to wait around for those who cannot arrive on time. My early years as an angler taught me that time was time and that appointments are to be kept. I would have it no other way and, strangely enough, no one in recent years, as far as I can recall, has ever been late twice. I have the most punctual friends these days!

If those early years did nothing else for me they gave me a sense of responsibility. They taught me the meaning of the word conservation (though I do not always agree with some present so-called conservation policies); they taught me patience and tolerance, they brought me close to nature and made me appreciate the countryside and the great outdoors. They taught me to be observant, to keep an open mind and not accept blindly every rule of thumb laid down with regard to the catching of fish. They taught me to disregard the dogma, the folk-lore and the mumbo-jumbo which was, and to some extent still is, tied up with fishing, and they made me think for myself.

Most of all, however, they made me realise that you get just about as much out of fishing as you're prepared to put into it. Which is how it should be.

Two-Rod Tactics

My Uncle Joe used to let me fish with him sometimes when I was a boy, and I came to realise, after a while, that he was a man of sayings. He had a quotation for pretty well everything to do with fishing and while I didn't believe all of them to be gospel, I admit that there was often a lot of sense in them. It's rather like learning your nine-times-table, I suppose. When you've heard it enough times you never forget it. That's why I always remember Uncle Joe's profound and favourite saying about fishing with two rods.

'If the fish are feeding, my boy,' he would say, 'two rods are too many. And if they're not feeding, one's too bloody many!'

When you stop to think about it, these are pretty wise words, and they apply in nine cases out of ten today.

I know there are exceptions and that there are certain very slow and stationary types of fishing that can be practised with two rods. Carp fishing, legering with dead baits for pike, trolling with lures from a boat, are typical examples, and one's chances are theoretically increased by two to one in these particular situations. I doubt very much if it's a mathematical formula that really works, of course, but in the circumstances I feel you might just as well use two rods as one.

Both rods are set to catch the same victim in the same way. The bait may be different, of course, and in most cases the object of using two rods *is* to offer a choice of bait, but the methods are basically the same. With two identical outfits fishing two different spots with two different baits there has to be an improvement in one's chance, but the use of two rods falls down badly when it is hoped to get the best of two worlds. Like, for instance, trying to floatfish for roach with one rod and leger for bream or chub with the other. I tried it many times in my early fishing days and it hardly ever paid off. I could never watch a rod tip with one eye and a float with the other! Nor could I ever watch a float that was anchored and one that was trotting at the same time!

I have, of course, like a good many other anglers, picked up a bonus perch or bream by concentrating on my trotting tackle and leaving a lobworm out on the other outfit to fish for itself. A big lobworm doesn't need to be dealt with quickly, and if the anchored float is lying in the right spot you can sense its movement out of the corner of your eye and still have time to deal with it. But you can't do that sort of thing with crust cubes or other soft or small baits.

Even in still water, where you can put two floats out so that you can watch both of them together you can only really concentrate on one at a time, and as Uncle Joe said, if the fish are really feeding you can only handle one outfit, anyway.

I remember once saying that I could handle either two float tackles or two legers, but that I could never manage one of each, and I believed it until I had one of those memorable days at Tring when the bream were really 'on'. I was determined to knock out a big catch but I honestly spent more time baiting up my legers, casting them and striking them than I did catching fish! As soon as one outfit was out and settled, I concentrated on the second but at that point I invariably had a bite on the first one. I dropped everything and struck wildly, of course, and as you might expect, I missed, again and again. Now I don't know what possessed me that day but suddenly it became an absolute thing with me to get two outfits fishing. And in all truth I never managed it. All I did was waste a lot of good fishing time and miss a lot of good fish. Finally, in desperation I hurled the second rod up the bank, stopped being greedy and started to catch fish. I don't believe I ever used two rods, leger or otherwise, at Tring again. Nor, as far as I can recall, did I ever have another session with so many bites.

One situation where I believe it makes sense to use two different outfits is with pike fishing. The working up of a roach swim, especially in a river, does much to encourage pike into the area. Most match anglers can tell stories of intruder pike that have attacked their keepnets, taken fish off their hooks and generally ruined their chances. I am sure, too, that most other anglers have experienced similar happenings at some time or other, and I see a real *need* for the second outfit here. What puzzles me sometimes, however, is the fact that, with pike swirling and striking in the swim, many anglers still insist on putting out their second outfit twenty yards away! The object of using the pike outfit is to catch the pike that's causing the trouble, and the best place to fish for it is where it is known to be.

This whole procedure can, of course, be set to work in reverse. If the main object is to catch pike, it's not a bad idea to choose a known roach swim, go to work on it with maggots and groundbait and begin catching a few of them. Theoretically, the introduction of bait and maggots alone should be sufficient to stir the swim up and stimulate the pike into feeding. But it doesn't always work out that way. It's the obviously different behaviour of the hooked roach that causes the pike to react as they do.

My Uncle Joe, along with other anglers of his day, would often say that the best way to catch pike was to go roach fishing. And he was right.

But he also had another saying. It was largely based on one single experience but he stood by it rigidly: 'If the pike aren't feeding,' he would say, 'throw stones at your float!'

On one occasion he had thrown in some deadbaits at the end of a fruitless day's pike fishing and had stood by helpless while pike struck at them immediately they hit the water. 'It was the splashing that did it,' he said. 'So now I throw stones to create the same effect.'

I tried it more than once in my youth but I only recall one time when it worked. On that day, a pike I could see—a small one—was eyeing my only remaining bait. I hoped for a bigger fish so I hurled a stone at the pike hoping to scare it away. It scared it off all right—but it grabbed the bait en route and dragged it into the rushes!

Nevertheless, there's something to be said for Uncle Joe's theory, and I can tell of numerous occasions when the disturbance caused by heavy spoons entering the water has triggered pike into picking up strategically placed deadbaits. It was once a regular practice to cast spoons and spinners through the area occupied by the livebait. The splash or the disturbance they caused was designed to attract the pike to the livebait and, according to Bickerdyke, Jardine and others, it used to work well enough.

Today the action of our modern lures is so good that they are just as likely to be taken as the live or deadbait. Which is one more good reason for making use of a second rod occasionally.

Natural Harvests

Most of us, whether we're coarse fishers, trout fishers or sea fishers, are interested in what fish eat. We make a fair study of what's on the menu for carp, tench, trout or mullet, and we try, very often, to offer them something that's available to them naturally.

We see a black fly hatching on the trout stream or reservoir and we try to offer an artificial that's somewhat similar. We know that tench eat mussels and so we use mussel hookbaits. We watch pike tearing into the rudd shoals and we offer them a live rudd, a dead rudd or a lure that looks like a rudd in the hopes that it will be good enough to fool them. It's true, of course, that we also offer fish bread and maggots which are not strictly part of their natural diet, but we know from experience that fish like them. It's a safe bet that, on some heavily fished waters, maggots have been accepted as part of their natural diet, and there are many who believe that the fish suffer severe hunger pangs during the close season because of the lack of maggots! They may be right.

I've always been interested in what fish eat, and if there has ever been any way in which I could offer the fish something similar to that which they were taking at the time, I've done so. I've caught dace on crane flies, perch on minnows and roach on elderberries because I've known that, at the time in question, these items of food were strictly on the menu and abundant. And I know very well that I would have stood very little chance of success with any other bait on those days. It so happened that the fish were having a bonanza with a very easily acquired food supply and they were interested only in that particular food at the time. I am not alone in this, of course. Thousands of anglers have met the same situation and cashed in on it just as I have done.

I recall one autumn some twelve or so years ago when a number of wheat stooks were washed into the river by an early flood. They settled in a great heap among the rushes upstream of a wide, deep bend and for several weeks there was an accumulation of roach and dace hanging around the area. We caught very few of them, they were too well fed, but those we did catch were only interested in wheat baits. We caught them on stewed wheat to begin with, and later, as was to be expected on single grains that had been merely soaked. We'd never had too much success with stewed wheat baits there before but we used it later that year and the following summer to good effect. As a 'minnow avoider' it turned out to be excellent, and although we probably thought that the stooks had been the start of their 'education' on to wheat baits, I wonder now if we'd have caught just as many roach if we'd persevered with them earlier. Later experiences seemed to suggest that this would have been so.

Finding out what fish eat naturally can help considerably in planning a season's fishing and it is as well to remember that fish as well as humans have natural harvests.

There's a great overhanging bush on the north bank of a lake I sometimes fish with my brother Ken, and most years there's a natural harvest of small caterpillars for the rudd to reap. The lake is huge, but there are always accumulations of rudd in this particular spot while the harvest is on. And, of course, it doesn't end with rudd. After a while the tench turn up to investigate. I doubt very much if they get many of the pickings because the rudd are too numerous and too active, but, just as carp will swim up to investigate surface rudd activity around a floating crust, so do the tench turn up here.

Occasionally, if we hit the right spot at the right time, Ken and I catch an odd one from the bottom right below the bush. Then, of course, the pike put in an appearance. Such activity cannot go on for long before they, too, join in and that usually puts an end to it all, but it's nice to cash in on this 'natural groundbaiting' while the opportunity arises.

In vast waters it is extremely difficult to attract and hold fish for long periods without using an enormous amount of groundbait over a very long time. No ten anglers could carry enough groundbait to hold some of the big bream shoals I have seen, and without some extraordinarily large accumulation of natural food to keep them occupied they are gone within minutes of occupying the swim. So is all the groundbait!

It would be interesting to see what the main food supply of bream consists of and I have said that one of these days I shall kill one and find out. But I know I'll never do it. And I doubt if it would help me if I did. Bream are great wanderers and cover large areas cleaning up as they go. It's unlikely that I'd find enough evidence to pin them down to one area or learn anything definite about their feeding habits, diet, or behaviour.

It might just be possible to tie them down in a situation similar to that which we met at Beaver Lake in America one year. It won't ever happen, of course, but it's interesting to speculate on just how a big bream would react to a continual supply of fish offal. Hundreds of fish are cleaned and gutted daily on the dock at Rocky Branch and the bones, livers, roes, guts and heads are dropped into the twenty feet of water off the edge. Lying full stretch, I have peered into the clear water and watched the shapes of huge carp and catfish feeding on this very regular and very abundant harvest, and I can readily understand why American carp take fish roes and livers so readily in this and other similar areas. I reckon there would even be enough food there to hold the interest of an English bream shoal!

Great accumulations of food, whether they be natural or unnatural, obviously have a bearing on the feeding behaviour of fish and fish shoals. That's what groundbaiting and pre-baiting are all about. We can also occasionally learn something from the contents of individual fishes' stomachs. The trout angler with his marrow spoon can, in fact, find out what the trout he's just killed was eating before it died—if that's of any use to him. There's nothing to suggest that all the other trout are feeding on it too and, as he managed to catch the first one anyway without that knowledge, I wonder why it's so important.

I always remember someone (I believe it was Ted Holiday) writing years ago that big rabbits sometimes ate little rabbits but that didn't mean that little rabbits were part of the big rabbit's diet!

I thought about that the other day when I went trout fishing. Inside one of the two-pound rainbows I caught I found two large snails, a partly digested frog and a whole gob of frogspawn. And believe it or not I caught that rainbow on a little green nymph. In one of the others was a white stone as big as a walnut and absolutely nothing else at all. Much good a marrow spoon would have done me that day!

Learning About Lures

'Is there any future in using artificial lures for coarse fish in this country?' That question can almost be guaranteed to come at some time or other during a club social evening, and I have grown to expect it. I welcome it because it usually develops into a really interesting discussion.

More and more these days I believe that coarse fish, other than the accepted predator, can indeed be caught on artificial lures and I sincerely believe there is some future in it. It is something which we, bait-fishers in the main, have not understood and have never even considered, but the field of artificial lures is a very wide one and, of course, it embraces flies and other creations which are still referred to as flies even though they bear no resemblance to insects at all.

The truth is that it is possible to imitate almost any form of live food taken naturally by our resident coarse fish and it has been proved many times in recent years by the number of accidental catches of coarse fish from fly-only reservoirs. If these catches had been made on flies tied to represent insects or nymphs they would not have been of great interest, but there have been many catches made on flies tied to represent minnows, perch fry, sticklebacks and even completely non-existent species of small fish.

We have known for a long time, of course, that all fish are predatory and that they almost certainly feed on other, smaller fish at some time or other during their development. Continental anglers at one time developed a method of spinning for roach and roach hybrids with very fine lines and tiny spoons. They may still practise it for all I know, but although it was sometimes discussed in this country, very few anglers ever tried it because many of our waters were unsuitable.

Since then, of course, a great deal of progress has been made and much more is known about the dressing and fishing of lures on the trout reservoirs. These fur, hair and feather creations are, of necessity, fished with fly rods and have accounted for roach, rudd, bream, perch, pike and hybrids as well as trout from the big waters where they co-exist. But they do not have to be fished with fly rods in order to be successful. Short-sighted fishery rules at present insist on making a mockery of the whole business by forcing anglers to use outfits not necessarily of their own choosing. I believe that is wrong on a public water. I will always consider it to be so despite my liking for fly fishing and the certain knowledge that often it is the most effective method.

Fly lures can be fished very successfully for coarse fish a number of other ways and it is interesting to round up some of the catches that have been made on them.

My brother Ken and I have taken roach, rudd, dace, chub, perch, zander, pike, grayling, eels and bream on lures ranging from hair streamers to Polystickles. I have had reaction—interested reaction—from carp, and I am confident that I will catch a carp that way eventually. Dick Walker has caught a whole lot of tench on fly-fished nymphs, and American anglers are taking carp that way too. These are what might be termed entomological lures but they are nevertheless artificial. Dan Gapen of Minnesota is now taking carp regularly on artificials which bear no real resemblance to any living insect or underwater creature. He refers to them as 'Ugly Bugs' and thinks it is possible that carp may take them for crayfish. These carp, in the upper Mississippi, live, incidentally, in fairly fast water and they may be more accustomed to taking food on the move than carp in still water.

There is a case on record of an angler trotting a Polystickle through a swim on float tackle and taking enough dace to win a match. My non-fishing brother, Dennis, caught roach and rudd on offset spoons during one memorable light-hearted spinning session.

I could go on giving instances of coarse fish other than the accepted predators being caught on artificial lures, and I am confident that we could make progress in this field if we persisted. In fact, we have already.

It is not easy to convince a dyed-in-the-wool bait fisherman that casting and working lures will attract and catch fish, mainly because he has to have confidence in whatever he is doing, and lure fishing, practised blindly, does not inspire that confidence. But if you can see the fish, and if you can get a lure to it without it seeing you, then the whole deal becomes more exciting. If you can see (as I have seen many times) a chub, rudd, carp or other coarse fish swim up to and investigate a bumping, bouncing, brightly coloured lure and watch its reaction, you will know immediately that here is a different way to catch fish. It will never replace bait-fishing for sheer efficiency, but it is, at times, undoubtedly more exciting and interesting.

I have sat and teased fish for hours at a time without inducing them to take, but also *without scaring* them. That seems to me to be important, because dropping an edible bait in front of a coarse fish often scares it into bolting. There is a lot to learn about suitable conditions and so forth, but I believe if we studied lure fishing more we would come to accept it as a regular method in time. It is one of the many subjects to consider when practical fishing is out of the question, but our close season is too short to do more than give it a passing thought.

Keep It Dark

When, years ago, I caught my first largemouth bass on a fly in Illinois, USA, I was so impressed with the fly, given to me by a friend in Minnesota, that I brought several of them back to England hoping to use them as trout flies. In Minnesota they had proved deadly for bluegills, crappies, perch and even the occasional small pike. Rainbows, I thought, would eat them up. On my return I promptly forgot them, and they did not see the light of day again until a year later when I returned to Illinois. Again they proved deadly and that same year I put them to use in England.

I was right. Rainbows fairly tore into them and pretty soon I was down to the last one. I wrote off to Minnesota immediately for new stocks and at the end of that trout season I gave the pattern to my brother Ken, who did his best to tie exact imitations. His dressings lacked the wisp of white elk hair contained in the American patterns, however, and, although they were highly successful flies, they were not quite up to the originals. I wrote again to Minnesota for a supply of flies, and to Illinois for a supply of elk hair.

Both commodities arrived but with the flies came a message: 'Don't spread them around, don't show them to too many people, and don't over-exploit them. If you do, they will end up by becoming just another lure. Remember what happened to the Swedish plugs? There was a time when they were unobtainable and retailers were, in fact *renting them out* for a dollar a day. Now that they are freely available, they have become just another lure. Excellent still, but no longer as deadly as they were. . . .'

There was more in the same vein, but I was not really interested in advice at the time. I had my flies and materials to make more, and as I had never believed in keeping secrets, I spread them around. I let one or two friends have samples and obviously they, in turn, showed them to *their* friends. Copies, not exact but close enough, began to appear, and a season later my deadly fly had indeed become 'just another lure'.

I was still reluctant to keep secrets about anything to do with fishing, but I have to admit that I was obliged then to give the matter some thought.

Working on the pattern of a black-and-white bucktail fly designed by Ted Trueblood and named the Integration, Ken and I came up with another incredibly effective streamer. It was shorter and more heavily dressed than the Trueblood version, but we still referred to it by its original name. And, more out of curiosity than anything else, we kept the secret to ourselves. If we lost a fly on the back cast, we searched until we found it. If we managed to put one up a tree (as we occasionally did) we moved heaven and earth to retrieve it. And as season succeeded season we made minor improvements to the original and made the Integration our number one choice.

I am not a very good fly caster. An old injury to a shoulder makes my casting erratic to say the least, and yet I can tell of many days when both Ken and I took limit bags at Little Tring within minutes, while others struggled on for hours. We were, I'll admit, very vague about what flies we were using, but I have no doubt that there are a few anglers who will read this and remember those days.

There was a period when, out of curiosity (or call it stubbornness if you like) I carried on fishing with the Integration during buzzer batches, and took my limit along with all the rest. During two seasons I hardly ever bothered to tie on another pattern. I had no need to do so.

Eventually, of course, we relented and told a friend what we were using. We swore him to secrecy and he, too, found that it was much easier to take his limit. He, naturally, told another friend, swearing *him* to secrecy, and that friend, in turn, told another and another.

Soon Integrations or 'black-and-whites' were in use all around the reservoir and what was once an incredibly effective fly became 'just another lure.' Today it still catches fish, but it is not the fly it once was.

I have yet to find another fly to equal it, but if I do I shall disregard my principles about secrecy and keep the knowledge to myself. But I think that is highly unlikely.

The more I think about this odd situation, however, the more I am convinced that my Minnesota friend's advice was sound. When Grafham Water first opened and Dick Walker publicised his Polystickle, limit catches on that fly were commonplace. Soon every tackle shop in the country began selling Polystickles and before too long it had become just another lure. It still catches fish today, but it is no longer the deadly creation it once was.

What, I wonder, makes a lure, fly or bait drop from grace so dramatically? And why does the message spread from water to water?

Some years ago a Texan (I believe) began hand-carving wooden plugs of a design completely different from any others in use at the time. He called his creation the 'Big O', and every bass fisherman in the USA began looking for one. Wherever they were used these plugs caught bass. Tournaments were won with them, and there was a time when many bass tournament fishermen regarded entering as a waste of time without a selection of Big O lures.

It was not long, of course, before similar mass-produced plugs began to appear. There was the Big This, the Big That, and the Big Whatever. Some had rattles incorporated, some were made with metallic and fluorescent finishes. One even winked its eyes when its immersion in water produced a current from a tiny battery! All caught bass for a period and then, like others that had gone before, they settled down into becoming just successful lures.

This strange happening almost certainly accounts for the secrecy involved in the production of new American lures. Most manufacturers attempt to bring out a new lure each season, but there is much cloak-and-dagger work done in advance, and 'field testers' are sworn to secrecy, while the new lures are not announced until they have proved successful. They are usually launched at the annual AFTMA Show when sufficient stocks have been built up to execute the big orders that follow.

On some of my trips to America I have been invited to 'field test' certain new lures, but always I have been asked not to 'make them public' before they were actually in the stores. In almost every case the lures involved were highly successful during field tests, and later became the season's 'hot lure'. The Gapen Ugly Bug was one such lure, the Burke Minno was another. Both were excellent smallmouth bass lures; both became (and to some extent still are because they are not readily available here) super lures for small English pike.

Familiarity, they say, breeds contempt. I wonder if fish become contemptuous of flies and plugs and spinning lures? Most carp anglers would agree that carp become, if not contemptuous, at least suspicious of baits after a few seasons. The once-deadly parboiled potato is, perhaps, no longer as effective as it was. It remains a good bait along with paste flake and breadcrust, but today's carp anglers are more secretive than those of yesteryear. Dick Walker, back in the early 1950s, advised us all that potatoes would become less acceptable after a few seasons and that it would be wise to wean the carp on to something different in the way of baits. How very true.

Now we hear of secret concoctions, secret baits, and secret this, that and the other. High-protein baits (some of which were, in fact, more carbohydrate than protein) ruled for a time. Maize, sweet corn, raisins, sultanas, baked beans, butter beans, green peas, trout pellets, pig pellets and other baits have had, or are still going through, their heyday. It is highly likely, despite the secrecy involved, that each in turn will settle into becoming just another bait. The mighty maggot is no longer the bait it was. Casters, hempseed, tares, and bloodworms—all have had their magic moments.

Today they are all accepted as good hookbaits, and excellent free feed, but they become increasingly less effective unless they are allied to the great skill and presentation of the dedicated matchman.

I am quite sure that it will continue to be this way. New flies, new lures, new baits, achieve success every so often. For a while they remain 'hot' but then, like others before them, they become very much run-of-the-mill, and then someone dreams up something different and better.

Well at least it keeps our brains active.

Smell Appeal

I used always to keep a diary, recording catches, conditions, companions, hours fished, and so on, in the hope that I could use the information compiled to assist in my future fishing. I tired of it eventually, however, and stopped keeping it when I became convinced that it was of no real help to me.

I doubt if these old diaries contain anything revolutionary, or if their contents could be allied to present situations and used to effect. But they do make interesting reading and bring back memories of little incidents long since forgotten. They remind me of ideas tried out in the past and make me wonder if they were as successful (or unsuccessful) as I imagined at the time. They stir little maggots of thought in my brain and give me the urge to try some of those ideas again.

I quote from a 1959 diary entry.

> Casting plugs around margins on lower lake. One surface plug with spinning head accounted for seven pike between 4 and 9 lb. Later, fishing deep-dive plugs, picked up a lost tackle armed with a well-worn plastic plug. Originally a floater this plug had been drilled and, judging by the smell, filled with pilchard oil. The smell was very noticeable and possibly indicated that the plug had only recently been lost. Is there anything to it? Is it worth injecting plugs or natural pike baits with strong smelling fish oil? Are pike likely to be attracted?

There had been evidence earlier that pike seemed occasionally to be attracted to strong-smelling sea fish such as herrings, and that, generally speaking, over a short period herrings had produced more runs than freshly killed rudd. Subsequent trials proved that there was no noticeable difference one way or the other, but for the time being it seemed sensible to give some thought to the idea.

Nothing very scientific was tried. No accurate timings were involved, but after shopping around I managed to get some pilchard oil and doctored some deadbaits with it.

Records show that the following weekend produced nothing of note and that there was nothing to suggest that pilchard oil held any fatal attraction for the pike. The following weekend, however, was a bit more encouraging. The entry reads as follows:

> Heavy rain brought river over banks. Chub fishing off. Pike fishing at lower lake better proposition. Water very dirty with mud seepage from far meadow. Chances reduced. Spinning hopeless. Fished for six hours with herrings soaked in pilchard oil. Three pike—3 lb, 5 lb, and 11 lb. The only fish taken on both lakes that day as far as I can tell.

That little episode gave me confidence and suggested that in coloured or muddy water there was, perhaps, a case for using baits treated with pilchard oil; but there's no *real* evidence in any of my old diaries that the results they produced could be regarded with any degree of excitement.

Other entries regarding different fish and baits, however, indicate that there was a great deal to be said for stronger smelling baits in coloured flood-water conditions. Strong cheese was particularly effective, and entries in the diary show that chub were more than willing to take it in flood conditions. Reading through these old entries gives the impression that cheese (and particularly old blue cheese) was the flood-water chub bait par excellence. It probably was. But today I often wonder if it was because it was a bait we used more than all the others put together. Did it succeed because of sheer fishing pressure? We'll never know for certain, but it's important to be confident in a bait and confidence usually makes you fish longer and more efficiently, which in itself helps improve the odds.

I have friends who are really working hard with pastes made up of trout pellets and bread. They are catching their fair share of chub and are themselves convinced that their special 'high-protein' baits are the cause of their success. I won't argue too much one way or the other, but I've a feeling that their angling skill and ability, allied to their knowledge of the water concerned, has something to do with it too.

I cannot deny, however, that they *have* done very well with this concoction when the water has been high and dirty, and it may well be true that their smelly baits are working as well for them as smelly cheese worked for me in the past.

It is strange, however, that, while I have great faith in that kind of bait in summer, I had no real success with it last winter.

One summer, when levels were low and fish like tench easier to locate, I proved beyond any doubt in my own mind that there was a certain magic about pastes made up from trout pellets and brown bread. I won't say I broke any records or did any great deeds, but I did find that tench were attracted to loose feeding with sinking trout pellets and that hookbait paste portions, made up to look as nearly as possible like the real thing, were taken readily once the swim was worked-up. And I'm fairly certain that the smell of the fish meal contained in the trout pellets helped draw the fish and put them in feeding mood.

Several times, a couple of years ago, I caught pike on plastic worms which I fished hard on the bottom. Not stationary, of course, but slowly on the move to make them appear lifelike and attractive. I used those worms because they could be attached in such a manner that they simply could not become snagged. I missed fish on the strike and I also had fish come off, but I caught enough pike on them to be sure that they worked.

A later experience with those same worms, however, set me wondering and put my thoughts on a new tack temporarily. One of them was picked up by a pike while it was lying still on the bottom. Or at least I *think* it was lying still. There's just a chance that the slight movement of the anchored boat was making it move fractionally on the bottom.

These plastic worms are buoyant. They float. The weight of the hook, if it is small and thin-wired, does not take them down directly to the bottom, and an uptrace lead of any kind anchors them so that they rise up that much from the bottom. On the day in question a small shot on the hook had anchored mine firmly (or so I thought) on the bottom and the bite which took place while I was attending to another item of tackle was a pick-up-and-run bite. I should point out that I was *not* fishing that way by intent and that the bait was only lying on the bottom temporarily while I did something else. I doubt if it would prove to be very profitable fishing with one of these worms lying still for a long period. But there is this to it: they *do* have a smell. It is mainly one of liquorice —but there could be other flavours added, such as aniseed; and one wonders if this smell or flavour plays any part in attracting such fish as pike.

Some of these worms are brilliantly coloured, others are drab and would be almost invisible in dirty water. But I sometimes find myself wondering if the combination of bright colour *and* attractive smell might just make spinning in flood water that much more rewarding. It's sheer guesswork, of course. I've never worked on the idea because I'm convinced that real fish baits are still the best answer to coloured-water pike fishing. But I *do* like to use spinners and plugs for pike, and if there's a chance of improving their effectiveness by adding a bit of smell to them, perhaps it's worth a try.

Trouble is I haven't much more time left, and I'm really hoping the water will fine down enough during the final days of the season for the pike to be able to *see* what I'm putting in front of them.

The Close Season

Recent discussions have shown that the coarse fish close season is still as controversial as ever.

I could think up a score of reasons why we shouldn't have one, but the main argument I'd have to use would be the fact that it doesn't do what it's supposed to do—that is, protect coarse fish stocks. It overlaps badly. Some pike have been known to spawn before 14 March. Some carp and tench have been known to spawn after 16 June. Bream are often seen spawning during the first week of the season. But, of course, in the strictest and over-simplified sense, our stocks do not need protection. In the main we don't kill coarse fish (though some of us reserve the right to kill the occasional pike for the table) and it could be argued quite logically that therefore there's no need to protect our stocks.

Further to this argument could be added the simple observation that you don't often catch fish when they're spawning. That part is true enough. Ask any carp or tench angler if he has ever found a fish interested in food while it was actually spawning. I know I have sat several times on 16 June and watched great carp wallowing, driving and actually spawning and nothing I could offer them was of the remotest interest. The truth, I dare say, is that they never even noticed any of it.

So it has been with tench. Two years ago I had a swim so well baited that tench were almost queueing up waiting for me to arrive. A great netful of stale loaves was disappearing daily and the water was muddy with tench activity. This carried on right up to 15 June—and on that night before the opening, the mesh was still full of bread. The tench had chosen to go off and spawn, and no amount of food could possibly cause them to change their minds. A few days before that I could surely have caught tench until I tired of it. As it was, the season opening coincided with their actual spawning time.

It *is* just possible (and I have done it myself) to tempt bream when they're on spawning beds. I don't believe they take a bait because they regard it as food, but rather because it somehow irritates them. One factor that leads me to think this way is that, very often, in these circumstances, a bait lying on the bottom is ignored, whereas one sinking slowly under its own weight is taken.

But whichever way you look at it, whether or not you believe fish can be caught in the act of spawning, there's surely precious little credit in it. I'm not very proud of the bream I've caught on the spawning beds except where the season has been exceptionally late and the fish only just getting ready to spawn. I've seen bream leaking spawn in August, however, and there's nothing enjoyable about catching a male bream that squirts milt all over you as you remove the hooks.

The present close season, unfortunately, doesn't prevent that from happening with all species of fish. Some of the bloated female pike we sometimes catch during the last few days of the season are certainly not in the best of condition, but they're legal.

The arguments about coarse fish protection do not stand up to such logic. If we put our fish back anyway, and if we can still find them spawning during the open season, what's the point? Any good lawyer could win such a case hands down. But is that the end of it? Do we really want to see a season without end?

Let's forget the logic for a moment and think in terms of angling pleasure, which is really the name of the game.

I have spoken to a number of coarse fishermen who have exploited enclosed waters during the close season and without exception they've told me 'It isn't the same'. Legally, or at least one assumes so, they were entitled to fish, but they didn't really enjoy doing so out of the season.

'Are the fish any easier to catch?' I asked. No, I was told. There was no difference except a sudden awareness that winter techniques gradually gave way to summer techniques as the close season wore on. These anglers found, as I suspected they would, that the roach and rudd just didn't feed during the brief spawning period. That in itself didn't matter much, but I heard tales of what should have been prime roach shedding scales, and showing a complete lack of spirit *after* the spawning act had taken place. And, in my opinion, there is no sorrier looking specimen than a freshly spawned roach. And I know because, again, I have caught them on opening day in that condition.

Dick Walker, Peter Stone and I once opened the coarse fishing season on the River Tweed. We need not have waited for the 16th, of course, because up there it didn't apply. But we did so because we wanted any possible specimens to be recognised as in-season fish.

We caught plenty of roach in the deep fast water on the edge of one of the better salmon pools, but they were a sorry sight. Thin and flabby, their loose scales fell off in the landing net, and we realised that any attempt at compiling a big catch was out of the question. The few we kept for photographs on the first day put paid to any thoughts of bulging keepnets.

We began putting them back at once, and after the second day we looked elsewhere for our sport. We caught grayling, trout, perch and flounders, and in the lively shallows a mile downstream we found some smaller roach actually rising to flies. We had fun with those—they were a little better mended. On the other hand, some of the roach we caught on bait ought to have been well over two pounds—but in their present condition they were poor one-and-a-half-pounders.

I didn't enjoy catching those roach, and I'm quite certain that anyone who yearns for a year-round open season would feel the same way once he had caught some himself.

I've often felt that some of the river fishing I've enjoyed during March could easily have gone on for another few weeks. I've also wished many times that I could start fishing on 1 June or thereabouts. But isn't that also part of fishing? What of the anticipation? Surely the build-up to the next season is a source of pleasure in itself. 16 June has got to be a special day for every coarse fisherman and to take away the frustration of the close season would lead to a certain lack of enthusiasm.

I readily admit that, because I have access to trout, salmon and sea fishing, should I so desire, during the coarse-fishing close season, my fishing never really stops. And I also have to admit that for that reason 16 June doesn't mean quite as much to me as it did twenty years ago. Whereas then I spent my spare time looking in tackle shops, purchasing the many little odds and ends I needed for opening day, repairing tackle, changing lines and so on in anticipation of the big day, I now never seem to have the time to do it.

That, in some respects, is sad, but it is all the more reason for me to believe that the close season, despite its faults and fallacies, is something we ought to cling to. I've no strong feelings against certain waters remaining open as long as it is legal. I've no wish to exploit them myself any more than I want to go up to the Scottish lochs to catch big pike off the spawning beds in April. Whatever turns you on!

That is also another reason why I will not go to Ireland to fish for May tench. I'm very much aware that these fish are quite legal and there's nothing morally wrong in it, but I just don't want to do it. Somehow I'd hate to catch a record tench and then be told, 'Ah, yes, but that was an Irish tench and in the close season.' Even if my friends didn't say it, I know that's what they'd be thinking—it's a natural reaction.

Strangely enough, though certain enclosed waters remained open at one time throughout the close season in my home county of Buckinghamshire, there was never any mad rush for day tickets. I believe this was because the average angler accepts the close season in a sense other than the strictly legal one. I believe most match anglers would be sickened at the sight of roach shedding scales in their keepnet, and I'm sure the average specimen hunter likes it the way it is.

I believe all fisheries benefit from the rest; I do *not* believe (as someone once tried to convince me) that the fish would suffer hunger pangs when their weekly ration of bait and groundbait was withdrawn.

I know that coarse fishermen are 'confined to quarters' during what is often the most pleasant part of the year. I agree that it would be nice to be able to fish occasionally during that period.

But I don't think we'd really enjoy our fishing any more if we could go as and when we liked. But there's nothing to stop us going to the water just to look.

The truth, of course, is that there's no need for anyone to stop fishing these days. If your only interest is in getting out with a fishing rod to try and outwit a few fish, there's nothing to stop you. Trout fishing undertakings in profusion are in competition with each other trying to attract you to them, and there's no reason why such waters should not be enjoyed to the full. Many coarse fishermen have quickly adapted and are now enjoying the best of both worlds.

As for me, apart from trout fishing, I like to potter around coarse fisheries during the fence months. It's nice to see the grass and herbage growing back over some of the rubbish left behind by anglers during the previous season. I dread to think what the banks of some waters would be like if they were used for the full twelve months without a break.

Horses for Courses

Part of my close season's activity involves tackle making and the creation of new fishing rods. I use the word 'creation' because if you asked me to do the mathematics and put it all down on paper, I could not design a garden rake, much less a fishing rod. That does not exclude me from being *involved* in rod design, however. I have a happy knack of being able to decide by feel and by field trials what should or should not be done to a prototype to improve it and make it suitable for the job—from my own point of view, that is. I am also able to co-operate closely with Dick Walker, who really can put it all down on paper and come up with the right answer. It is surprising just how near to the right tool you can get at the first attempt when two of you have the same idea in mind.

The development of new rods and tackle, and the general improvement of equipment due to new and better materials will, of course, continue. There are better things in store for us in years to come, and I am all for that, but I have to agree with some of the sentiments expressed in recent years regarding the development of specialist tackle and equipment.

Without bringing personalities into it at all, and speaking purely from my own observations, I believe that there are times when more attention is paid to the tackle than to the fish being sought. And there is a tendency to follow blindly any lead in the field of tackle development which proves successful for a certain angler on a certain water at a certain time.

It is almost as if those concerned believe that here, at last, is the answer to all their problems. With this new rod, reel, float, bite alarm or whatever, they are suddenly going to catch fish. It does not work that way. The sad part about it is that in many cases the item of tackle has been developed for a particular purpose and as such is not suitable for more general situations. Those who buy and use these items could easily put themselves at a disadvantage and the chances are that they would do just as well with the equipment they already have.

The truth is that many of these longer, stiffer, more powerful, faster, etc., etc. kind of rods are excellent for what the designer or improver has in mind. But to continue along those lines and to make them even longer, stiffer, more powerful, faster, and so on and so forth, is not always very clever. There comes a time when everything becomes out of proportion, and this undoubtedly takes a great deal of the pleasure out of the fishing.

If someone designs a pike rod for fishing in, say, Loch Lomond or a similar water, where the possibility of a fifty-pounder is ever present, that is a specialist rod. It has been thought out with due consideration to that situation, and the size of the fish hoped for is but one of the factors considered. Other necessary considerations are, of course, the underwater geography, the snags, the amount of space available to play a big fish and so on.

A rod of this nature would probably have to be designed to hold a multiplier loaded with 20–30-pound test line, and its test-curve might be in the region of 4 pounds. So, although this rod might prove to be the world's greatest whopper-stopper, its advantages would be lost on an open, snag-free water where fifteen-pounders are rare and the average weight of pike is around half that.

A whopper-stopper rod can't stop whoppers where none exist, and I believe it is better to study the water and its potential than to devote so much time and money to the development of rods that are unnecessarily powerful.

Having been interested in rod design for some years (again I stress not as a mathematician but as a practical angler) I have seen a great deal of development along the lines already mentioned, and my thoughts these days are concerned more with the soft approach. I have tried to think in terms of rods that give the most pleasure in normal situations and I have had a lot of fun with moderate-sized fish like six-pound carp and pike on short limber rods that let me know there is something on the other end. How many times, I wonder, have small pike been cranked in on powerful rods without so much as a kick to let their captors know anything about them?

We cannot all catch enormous fish because we cannot all fish waters where they are known to exist. It is true, I know, that some waters hold bigger and better fish than many anglers suspect, but very few of them demand tackle developed to record-breaking standards. So I believe it is better to exploit the average fishing to the full and use tackle that gives the maximum pleasure while still offering a better than even chance against an unusually big fish, should one be hooked.

There are, of course, waters where the really important factor is casting distance. They are quite rare in my part of the world but these waters can be fished better with rods capable of casting baits a long way. The design of such a rod may, however, reduce its other capabilities. It may be inconvenient in other ways, but if the catching of fish depends entirely on long-range casting, it is obvious that the rod has to be up to scratch in that respect.

It is also worth remembering that a rod designed to punch a lead out sixty or seventy yards is a different proposition from one designed to cast a piece of soft paste. Whichever way you look at it there has to be a compromise unless you are prepared to sacrifice one quality for another.

There never will be a rod capable of doing everything to absolute perfection, but I am convinced that the need for super-specialist rods is limited to specialist anglers fishing specialist waters, and that average waters are better fished with average tackle.

I have helped to develop an ultra-light glass rod which I find myself using more and more for all kinds of fishing. The action could only be described as 'sweet', and its length is just over nine feet. I have used it for sensitive touch legering (for which it is superb), light spinning for pike, floatfishing for tench, free-lining for carp, and trotting for dace. I have caught lots of fish of over ten pounds with it and it still gives me plenty of action with a four-ounce roach. It will never serve as a brute-stick for a thirty-pound pike in snaggy water, it will not cast a hundred yards, and it will not throw a dead bait weighing half a pound, but it is the nearest thing to perfection I have ever handled as far as general, non-specialist fishing goes. It is capable of doing more than most of the other rods I own, and I am very happy with it. I do not want to make it longer or stiffer or faster or whatever. If I did I would be limiting its use to special situations and losing a lot of my fishing fun.

I find this preoccupation with bigger and stronger tackle or equipment boring and will have none of it.

My landing net has 36-inch arms and a 48-inch deep mesh. I cannot think of any fish swimming in British fresh waters that is likely to be too big for it. And yet I am asked a hundred times a season where to obtain landing net frames with arms measuring forty-eight, fifty-four and even sixty inches! I swear that half the time these fellows only want to own a net bigger than their friends.

And so it goes on all through the trade. A top match angler wins a big Open using a certain float, and you can be sure that float will be in demand and used in the most unlikely situations for the next few weeks.

I once caught a twenty-pound pike for Nationwide Television on a big lightweight spoon, and I happen to know that the sales of that spoon rose tenfold during the month that followed. There is absolutely nothing wrong with the spoon. It is still a great fish-catcher, but I chose it to exploit a special situation on the day. Many anglers used it afterwards to good effect, but some used it, or tried to use it, where it was of little use. I saw one angler beating himself to death trying to cast it into the wind at Tring a few days later. He told me he was using it because he'd seen it on TV and that if it worked then it should work now. He would have fared a lot better with a heavy, streamlined spoon that he could have punched out into the teeth of the wind because it just so happens that this big lightweight model simply cannot cope with those conditions.

'Horses for courses,' someone once told me, 'applies particularly to fishing.' He was right, of course.

Some people would enjoy tackling the Grand National with a suitable mount; others might prefer to jog along through farmland on a steady old nag. Neither one could be considered superior to the other in terms of pleasure, and it would be foolish to try and change them round. Which is exactly how it is, or how it should be with regard to fishing and fishing tackle. And we should take time out to think about it sometimes during our close seasons.

Visible Chub

There was a time when I reckoned that the most difficult part about chub fishing was finding them, and I was almost (but not quite) arrogant enough to think that if I could find 'em I could always catch 'em.

There are chub and chub, of course, but when you stop to consider the many different ways of catching them and the number of different situations in which they can be found, I believe that, in the long run, chances are naturally increased if you can actually see the fish. The chances of frightening them away are increased too, of course, and this obviously has to be taken into consideration.

I am reminded if this generally accepted chub lore by two recent close-season happenings.

I have spent many hours in years gone by watching, scheming and dreaming up ways of catching chub during the opening weeks of the season, but lately I've spent so much of my close-season time fishing for trout, salmon and the odd sea fish, that I've tended to neglect these important preliminaries. Sheer chance—a traffic diversion, in fact—took me across country the other day and I found myself back in surroundings I had almost forgotten. The two little streams that pass under the road before meeting up to join the main river were low and clear, but otherwise they looked no different, and I remembered that here was where I'd caught my first ever chub—a fish of about 2¼ pounds so many years ago. Then I remembered those bigger fish I'd seen (and occasionally caught) downstream later and I had to go and look for myself once again.

I had absolutely no authority to be on the land and, as I am no longer a member of the club controlling the water, I asked at the farmhouse if I might walk the meadow. The reaction was one of surprise because apparently few people had ever had the courtesy to ask before, but permission was readily granted and I took my walk.

It was almost as if time had stood still for twenty years. There, where the chub always used to lie, were seven big fish. Restless, patrolling near the surface, idling briefly in the slow current and dropping back into the shadows of the bulrushes. They did not see me, I'm quite sure of that, but I'm also quite sure that I could not have caught these fish at that time. Later in the day, perhaps, early the following morning, maybe, but these were fish not in the feeding mood, and I doubt if they could have been stimulated into feeding.

That's not to say, of course, that visible chub cannot be tempted during the middle of the day. They can; and the success or otherwise of the operation depends upon the *mood* of the chub and the angler's ability to fool them into grabbing a bait without stopping to think. (If fish *can* think that is!)

Generally speaking, the only real requirement is that you should be able to get a bait to the fish without it seeing you or being scared by your approach in any way. Most of the time it works, but there are times when, despite all caution, and the absolute knowledge that they have not been scared, chub will *not* react in the accepted manner. And, if you've done much chub fishing of this kind, you can nearly always tell. There's a difference in their movement; a subtle difference that cannot easily be explained or described, but in these circumstances their reaction is *not* to investigate an offered bait, *not* to turn swiftly and greedily to engulf it, but to back cautiously away. There's no panic, no hurried departure, just a suspicious and apparently irritated back-off.

I recognised that situation the other day. I recognised, too, that the season was well forward and that this behaviour was something I'd normally expect to see here and there during the opening weeks. And I recognised the difficulties those fish would have presented had I been in a position to fish for them there and then.

These were a random gathering of chub, not strictly members of the same shoal, but fish that had somehow been brought together by circumstance, and if you have ever seen such a gathering you will know what I mean when I suggest that they are not a *happy* gathering.

Back in 1960 I wrote: 'If you can see a chub and carefully cast a bait to him without showing yourself—he is as good as yours.' Then, I was writing of a single chub, and I believe those words still apply today.

I qualified my remarks, however, by mentioning the situation where a number of chub, obviously not of the same 'brood' had gathered together more or less by accident. 'They move in a haphazard way,' I wrote. 'And in no wise do they follow the typical shoaling instinct. They roam aimlessly . . . and almost appear distressed with each other's company. Later these groups break up . . . .'

There is undoubtedly less water in the little river today, the chub are smaller and their numbers fewer, but their habits and their general behaviour seem to have changed little. It was pleasant to see those fish, to spend a little time with them and to feel fairly confident that what I'd written all those years ago would still stand up today.

The second incident took place when I was trout fishing on another small stream and where chub are strictly out of favour.

I'd never before seen more than one chub in a lie there and, in fact, there are very few anywhere along the whole reach at any time, but on that day I spotted three together below an overhang of willow.

It's the sort of place you'd expect to find a chub according to the old books but where for some reason they don't always appear to take up residence today. They were different fish in all respects from the others I'd watched. These were small (under two pounds), active and unconcerned. Each of them in turn followed my fly several times without taking, but I had the feeling that these were no suspicious refusals but completely uninterested ones. I dragged a streamer fly past them several times but could not stimulate them further, and as my main concern was trout anyway I left them after a few more casts.

After lunch, with a couple of trout on the bank and confidence restored somewhat, I accidentally foul-hooked a minnow (which isn't surprising considering how thick the shoals are). At that point I remembered the chub and (lest my intentions should be misunderstood) I invited the keeper to join me in bringing about their downfall.

With fly rod, lightly dressed damsel fly nymph and dead minnow, we crept down to where they were lying and, from a vantage point above, I issued instructions as to where the minnow should be lowered.

It was fun-fishing pure and simple and I got a kick out of giving a running commentary on what was happening to my 'blind' partner.

By pinching a swan shot on to the hook (and completely ruining the dressing in the process) we were able to troll, in the true and old-fashioned meaning of the word. Slowly up and quickly down went the minnow and this action was just too much for an immature chub to resist. It took on the up-beat, and was struck and lifted out all in the same movement. A beautiful piece of rod-work that only a close observer such as I could appreciate.

The minnow was mangled but still serviceable so the procedure was repeated and yet another chub bit the dust of the dry bank within seconds. In the process the minnow was lost and that was an end to it, but there's no doubt in my mind that we'd have nobbled all three if we'd been really out for blood.

Here was a typical see-'em-and-catch-'em situation. Three fish all much about the same size and apparently happy to lie and feed together. So different from the accidental accumulation of fish discussed earlier. And so much easier to catch, of course—a point worth remembering when the season proper opens.

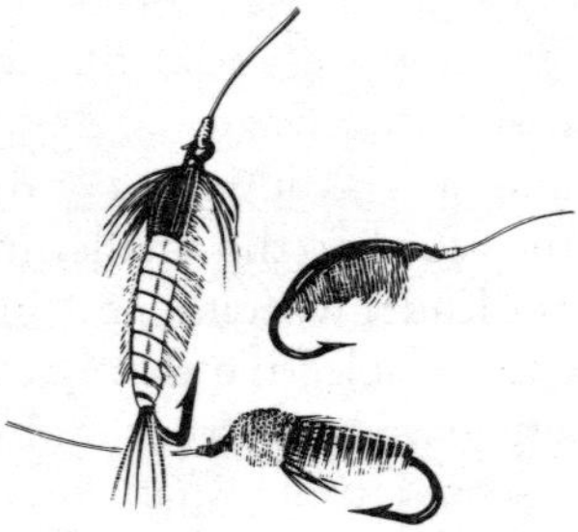

A Piscatorial Puzzle

Do you reckon fish know the date? You'd think they did sometimes according to the way they behave, and it's amazing to me how things can suddenly change between, say 14 and 16 June.

I spend a lot of time watching and weighing up prospects during the close season and there's no doubt I've learned a great deal about fish behaviour in general because I do, but there's no explanation for some of the things that go on.

Fish are a law unto themselves, of course, but what's the name of the law that says 'Irrespective of what the fish are doing on 15 June, they will *not* be doing it twenty-four hours later'? (I know what it's called, of course, but I doubt if the publisher would print it.)

Seriously though, I usually manage to open the season reasonably well because I make up my mind in advance what I'm going to do and where I'm going to be, but there have been times when I've changed plans and come unstuck.

I'm reminded of it all because I walked the banks of a favourite stream just a short while ago and spotted a great shoal of chub. It was headed by a big fellow, probably in the five-pound-plus class, and none of the fish seemed to be particularly bothered about my being there. They knew the date, or they knew I hadn't a fishing rod with me.

I recalled what happened in the same spot some fifteen years ago. The river was deeper then but just as overgrown and just as clear. The chub were bigger on average but they were shoaled in the same spot and behaving just about the same.

On that occasion we scratched around and found some worms to throw to them, and it was interesting to see the way they reacted. Right from the word go the smaller members of the shoal got to the worm first; the leader was either not interested or cautious. Even when we tried to be selective there was no way of doing so. The little ones were always up front and it wasn't until we'd fed the shoal for some time that the big fellow took one.

I'm reminded here of something the late Dave Carl Forbes once said—that it's darn near impossible to be selective with regard to chub. You can sometimes bounce a bait on a big chub's tail and nail it before it realises it's reacted too quickly but, generally speaking, it's difficult. There's no way of doing it consistently.

If any of the loose worms we used had been attached to a hook we'd have caught just one of the smaller chub and the rest would have vanished. We went over several times during that close season and fed the chub bits of bread, cheese and worms. They were almost tame when we'd finished with them, but they simply were not there at all when we fished for them properly. They'd split up, disappeared up the creek completely and our best-laid schemes had gone with them.

As it turned out, that was the best thing that could have happened because we were able to winkle out one here and one there from the lies they'd chosen to inhabit instead. Had they been shoaled we'd have caught fewer fish, but I'm still puzzled as to why those fish suddenly changed the whole pattern of their existence. There was no obvious reason for it.

It's happened more than once and it's happened with fish other than chub.

I'll never forget the shoal of roach about 200 strong we spotted in early June one year. There were some near two-pounders present and I doubt if any one fish weighed less than a pound. We watched them for two weeks, marked them and planned how we could fish for them in comfortable concealment. (A big pike took up residence immediately below them at one stage so we fashioned a snare and removed it elsewhere—highly illegal I suppose, but no harm done, really, and our shoal of roach was saved.)

The shoal was still there on 15 June but incredibly there was not a fish to be seen the next day! Nor could we find any sign of the shoal elsewhere along the river. It will always be one of life's puzzles.

Just before the next season opens I shall go over to the stream and take a loaf of bread with me just to see if those chub will play the same game as before. I dare bet they'll eat the whole loaf without batting an eye and that whoever fishes for them on 16 June (it won't be me—I've been had before) will either find them missing, not interested in food, or scared half to death the moment he approaches.

I've always said it's a lot of fun to catch fish you can see. So it is. But because you can see them in the close season doesn't necessarily mean they'll be there when it opens.

For about four years Dick Walker and I went to watch a particular shoal of barbel on the Avon. It was always there around the big clay boulder, and it was even there when we were allowed to fish from 1 July onwards. We never really came to terms with those fish, however, because on or around 7 July each year they moved out, and although we located the odd fish occasionally elsewhere, we were never able to tackle them as we'd liked to have done.

Those were big fish. Some of them were undoubtedly record breakers, and the sad part about it all was that, given time to fish for them earlier, we would probably have been in with a good chance of catching one. At least you know you're in the right place if you can see the fish under your rod tip! But, fish being what they are, they'd probably have moved out after a few days anyway.

How many carp anglers, I wonder, have spent time watching carp during the close season and enticing them to take floating crust? It's still the most exciting way of carp fishing in my book and while I always take out insurance in the shape of some bottom feed too, I enjoy the time spent coaxing carp to the surface and normally regard it as time well spent.

You can't do it everywhere, of course. It seems that some carp do not respond to surface baits at all, but where there are lots of small rudd or roach present, they seem to catch on quickly.

I've sat on the jetty at my local pits and fed the fish night after night until I've had them almost feeding out of my hand. I've actually thrown lumps of wet crust directly to cruising carp and watched them swim over to suck them down without suspicion. But what I can't understand is why they suddenly become suspicious of floating crust the moment the season opens. I won't say they can't be caught, but there's no doubt at all in my mind that they've suddenly developed a caution they didn't have during the close season. And I know I'm not alone in this respect. Other carp anglers have told the same story many times.

Not that it's going to change my ways at all. I'm still daft enough to think that this year will be the one when things work out the way they should. And even if they don't, I can still enjoy creeping around banks and climbing trees to spot fish that I *hope* will still be there on 16 June. When I don't enjoy it, it will be time to quit!

Tadpole Revisited

When Pete Drennan and I went to fish for barbel at Tadpole Bridge, I realised that something like seven years had gone by since I last fished this popular, but productive, stretch of the Upper Thames.

Little had changed. The river was well up but not in heavy flood, and the morning was damp and misty. In the old days I'd have said it was a good barbel day and Peter reckoned it was too.

One change was very noticeable, however. The swim I used to call the Fence Swim was naturally still there, but it was no longer marked by a fence and the undercut vertical bank, which used to be its most attractive feature, had collapsed. Now there was a gentle slope and a well padded bank spot close to the water's edge. It didn't look much like a barbel swim any more and I passed it by with some regret. I had spent many happy hours there in the past and I had hoped to relive some old memories on that day, but now other spots looked more attractive.

Downstream, another angler was settling in for the morning and we chatted for a few moments before moving on. He was hoping for chub, he said, and recent experiences had suggested that he should do well with floatfished casters and a moderate amount of groundbait.

I recalled that in days gone by my brother Ken, cousin Joe and I used to fish there almost exclusively for chub and that we used breadcrust on short link-leger tackle to good effect. This was a prolific chub water and our tactics had been to keep on the move, taking a fish here and there. We seldom sat it out in one spot, and there was always a certain amount of competition for what we regarded as the most likely swims.

On one memorable day I took eleven chub up to nearly four pounds while a match was in progress on the opposite bank, and Joe, who returned with a beaming smile having caught only ten, was shattered. That was one of the very few times I ever managed to beat Joe at chub fishing, and at Tadpole Bridge it was a fairly safe bet that he would find fish when I didn't.

He had an idea that, when the water was thick and muddy,

it paid to roll his crust bait in the mud on the bank before fishing, and whether or not it made any difference, I'm sure that it gave him the confidence necessary to succeed in difficult conditions.

These were some of my thoughts as I tackled up on a swim chosen by Peter, but as he had already been informed that lobs were at the time the No. 1 bait, I cast one across and slightly down, letting it come to rest under the overhanging bank below. It seemed a perfect barbel situation, and I was further encouraged by the sight of the angler upstream already bent into one. He eventually landed it and brought it along to be weighed—six pounds, two ounces. He had taken it on floatfished caster 'dragging on'; he put it back at once.

Peter, despite his great floatfishing ability, used sausage paste on leger tackle just above me. He was in no mood, he said, to wade through the hordes of gudgeon that would surely come if he used loose feed and float tackle. The gudgeon would peck and whittle away at the sausage meat and he could resign himself to their whittlings, knowing that there would be no mistaking a barbel bite if it came.

A slow pull on the lob put me into business and, with a scrappy fish on the end I thought I had hooked a small barbel on my first bite of the day, but it turned out to be a run-of-the-mill chub.

We talked of the difference in bites and how it is possible, in some indefinable way, to tell barbel bites from others. We recalled the fabulous days we used to enjoy on the Kennet when legered maggots would produce gudgeon after gudgeon until the moment came when a bite, just that little bit slower and more defined, would allow us to say in advance that here at last was a barbel. It happened that way so many times, and the interesting point about that kind of fishing was that it rarely worked with float tackle. You could trot a maggot bait through all day and catch a mixed bag of roach, dace, chub and gudgeon without seeing a barbel. A light leger presentation, however, would almost certainly produce a barbel, and often a dozen or more, in a day.

Peter recalled that, in those days, we were set in our ways regarding floatfishing and that we were somewhat obsessed with the traditional Avon style of holding back to ensure that the bait preceded the float. We were not upsides with the shot-dragging techniques so successful today.

In the early days, Peter, as a very young man, had learned a little about general fishing from watching and talking to me. Today I learn something new from him every time we fish together. With his skill and enthusiasm he could almost certainly fish me into oblivion, but we tend to compare notes rather than compete.

We didn't get our barbel. We caught roach, chub, gudgeon and perch (again it was a delight to see them back), relaxed, drank coffee and talked.

A tiny fieldmouse poked its head through the long grass at Peter's feet. He fed it sausage meat which it devoured with complete disregard of his gumboot an inch away. We became temporarily more interested in fieldmice than in fish and eventually Peter picked the little fellow up and held it in cupped hands for me to inspect more closely. He received a nipped finger for his trouble (served him right) but after that it didn't seem to mind. When he released it it padded off, slowly disappearing into the long grass, and we wondered how long that fearless, somewhat foolhardy, little beast would survive. It was surely wide open to attack from the stoats, weasels, gulls and other predatory creatures along the banks. But perhaps it was smarter than we thought.

At The Trout, we talked with the landlord about the river. 'It hasn't changed much, Fred,' he said. 'The Fence Swim is still there even though the fence isn't, and although it's changed a bit, it still produces barbel and chub. It also produces some good quality roach, which it didn't before.'

Peter asked about the most likely barbel spots at this time of year and received, from the publican and others present, a detailed description of the two best swims. They were, in fact, the very two we'd chosen and it was gratifying to know that at least we'd been fishing the right spots for all our lack of success.

I would have been surprised, and I would have regarded it as a fortunate coincidence, if we had happened to drop on to the barbel at the first attempt. Despite having some previous knowledge of the water, I would expect to have to make several visits before coming to terms with the situation, and I would not hope to make any real impression until I'd fished there for at least a whole season. That, unfortunately, is something I can no longer do.

Nevertheless, at this moment, I regard the Thames as one of the best barbel rivers in the country. Friends who fish the upper reaches regularly catch good fish and, although double-figure specimens are not exactly lying thick on the ground, I think it's fair to say that, per hour fished, as many are turning up there as anywhere else.

There are many ideas at the back of my mind, many things I want to try, and I hope that time will allow me to put some of them into practice. Times have changed. The methods we used in days gone by are possibly less effective than the modern float and feeder methods use today, and barbel fishing in itself is, perhaps, somewhat different. But I believe that the principles of location are still the same. I am prepared to believe that the actual bait presentation is still as critical as ever and that the so-called hot-spots still exist.

I know many situations where a foot or so either way makes all the difference between bites and blanks, and I appreciate the fact that these critical spots take time to locate. Without the knowledge gained by sheer experience, it is all too easy to be presented with a 'hot' swim and lose out.

I have gone to a great deal of trouble many times to ensure that a guest has had the best swim on a fishery, and I've realised afterwards that giving him the best swim was not enough. I should have pointed out the hotspots as well.

Kind friends have done the same for me, and, because I have failed to read the water correctly, I have not been able to take real advantage of their generous offers. In time I'd have scratched around and put it all together, but one day is seldom enough.

When we used to fish week-long spells on the Avon, it took several days for us to come to terms, and we were usually just getting to know the drill when it was time to go home. I'd like to spend a similar week at Tadpole. Thames barbel present a rather special challenge, but I believe I could learn a bit more about their ways given time.

Well, they say it's a sad day when you don't learn something new about fishing and I learned a little wrinkle from the landlord of The Trout before I left, which I pass on for comment.

We were discussing deep and shallow landing nets and the advantages of one over the other in different circumstances.

'I always use a deep one,' said the landlord. 'I put a rubber band round it to shallow it up for use with smaller fish, but if I get a big 'un the band opens up and the fish falls into the deep mesh below it.'

Why, I wonder, didn't I think of that!

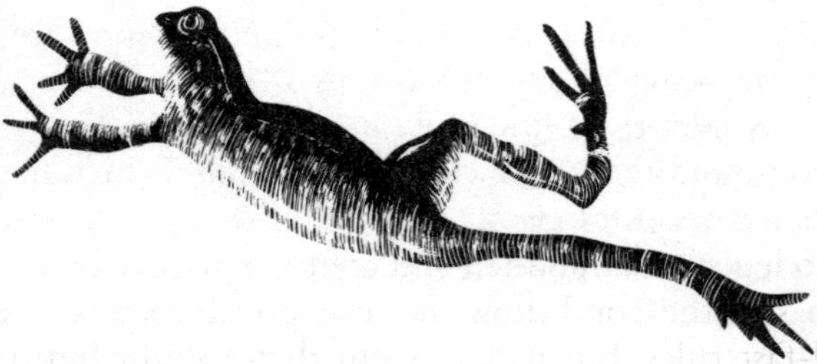

Colour Code

Floods upset fishing temporarily, but in the long term they do a lot of good. A great many waters fish that much better as soon as the level drops and the water clears, and I think it's sometimes very good for these changes to take place. Fish often react to such changes time and time again, whereas they may remain in dour mood during periods of no change.

I suppose I'm lucky in that I have access to two waters, very close to each other and part of the same river system, that respond to entirely different situations. One seems to hold very few fish at all in normal conditions, but often 'fishes up a storm' in flood. There are only a few productive spots, but they are typical flood-water swims and it seems that all the fish accumulate in these spots while the flood is at its height.

I've often sat on a big gravel bar (that is some yards away from the river's edge in normal conditions) and fished the back-up formed by the flood water. It's a clear water usually, but when the floods come down through the great clay plains of Buckinghamshire it goes disgustingly thick. I usually manage, however, to catch roach, dace, small chub and, occasionally, perch from the deep hole on the edge of the current. I'll qualify that by saying that the only exception is when the extra water comes from melting snow. Then I never catch anything.

I like this particular spot, a cut-off from a mill stream, because it provides me with a simple style of fishing in flood conditions. I don't know why this patch should fish well while other equally inviting spots a few miles distant produce nothing until the water subsides. But, of course, it's nice to be in a position to choose the water to suit conditions.

When the main river (the Ouse in its upper reaches a few miles away) drops, and the water clears, the fishing which has been so bad suddenly becomes good.

I like to leger for chub then and try to apply my baits and techniques to suit the conditions. It's not possible to lay down any hard-and-fast rules, but it does seem that a slight hint of colour in the water improves the situation. This is true of other rivers too, but it is also very much the other way regarding some of the chalkstreams I fish.

I've never found the Kennet, Avon or Test to be very productive unless the water has been clear but, of course, this is just my own experience. Some of the biggest barbel caught from the Avon and Kennet have come from deep, floodwater swims. Other anglers agree with me here, though, and I always remember the late Leslie Brewer, a fine barbel fisherman, saying that the Kennet was 'at its best when it sparkled'.

Nevertheless, a fining flood water has always been considered good for roach and chub fishing in the past, and I believe it's still the same today in many waters. Certainly our fish of the Upper Ouse respond better then, and at the time of writing, the chub fishing is at its peak. I haven't done much myself but friends have been having a ball.

Like me, they have found that slight changes in conditions have called for different baits and presentations, and they have found that chub are just as easily scared now as they are in summer in spite of the extra colour in the water. The only difference, of course, is that in summer you know you've scared them; in winter you're never sure. I believe in playing safe and assuming that they can see me all the time.

Some of the best chub I've ever caught or seen caught came in January and the differences in conditions that can come about between one weekend and another call for a great deal of angling adaptability.

The great thumping bites of last week may now be mere twitches or trembles on the line. Today, big lobs and chunks of cheese may be taken greedily; in a few days a tiny cube of crust may be the only successful bait.

It's not possible to tie it all down and give positive reasons, but I think it could be fairly stated that small baits will serve better when the water is cold, big baits are more likely to be taken when the water temperature is well up in the forties (degrees Fahrenheit), and baits with a smell (cheese, lobworms, luncheon meat, sausage, etc.) will prove more satisfactory in coloured water.

I'm very conscious of the fact that bites are likely to be more delicate, especially in heavily fished waters, and I'm sure it's very easy to over-feed chub in slower moving rivers. Even mild winter conditions are comparatively cold and in the main I think it better not to overdo the groundbaiting but to offer only a few hookbait samples where possible. I believe that the chub's apparent need for less food in cold weather relates to the manner in which it takes, and the size of the bait needed to catch it. And I believe that all this gives an indication as to what method should be used.

Look at it this way. Chub (we're talking about chub but it could apply to other species) move around slowly when the water is cold. I've had the opportunity in the past to study chub in certain uniform stretches of river, and I came to the conclusion that when they were moving around, chub would cover certain beats, back and forth, for several hours at a stretch. But whereas in mild weather they would cover the beat quickly several times, in icy-cold conditions they would travel slowly and, perhaps, confine themselves to the one excursion.

Then they would seemingly approach baits slowly, ignore large offerings and take small ones with extreme delicacy. In the cold they moved around very little so they needed little food, they moved around slowly and for that reason they took baits that were lying stationary on or near the bottom and ignored those that were fished either on long link legers or float tackle which allowed them to waver about in the current at different depths.

These fish did not chase baits, nor did they come up towards the surface for them; and the very fact that they did everything *slowly* meant that some of the bites could hardly be sensed.

It's the same today. Rod-tip bites are hardly noticeable at times, and I can recall many occasions when the only indication I've had was a slight twitch on the line where it entered the water. On other occasions I've been holding the rod when the only bite indication was a slight tremble or grating on the line between my fingers.

I do not know of *any* bite indicator that could have registered those bites. A very fine quivertip *might* have done so, but I doubt it.

I don't suggest for one moment that these are the only chub bites you can expect in winter, but I do suggest that you don't always wait for the big thump that bends the rod round in a quarter-circle. You'll get them occasionally, but you'll miss out on a lot of chub if you wait for them exclusively.

You get so many different kinds of leger bites from chub that you can be fooled into thinking they're from smaller fish or that they're not bites at all. That's why legering for chub demands more concentration than legering for most other species.

Very often, if the bait is out in a fairly lively current, the lead will be dislodged from the bottom and the line will slacken briefly before tightening up again downstream. This is usually caused by a freak build-up of the current, but *sometimes* it is caused by a chub picking up the bait. If you wait until the line is taut again the chances are that you'll be too late. It's that slackening of the line that presents the opportunity and that's when the strike should be made.

If the same thing happens in a certain spot every time you cast, of course, you can be sure that it *isn't* a bite; but where there is any doubt it pays to hit that slack line every time.

From all this you have to decide whether to hold the rod or whether to put it in rests. It's easy to say 'hold the rod all the time', but very often it's not a wise thing to do. It's fine if you're getting bites regularly and you're in action for most of the time hitting (or missing) fish, but when you have to wait perhaps an hour or more (and sometimes all day) for one bite, I think it's much better to relax with the rod in rests.

Obviously you have to decide whether you're going to *feel* for the bites or *watch* for them, and only you can make that decision with due regard to the water you're fishing and the conditions at the time. But when bites are few and far between I'm sure that my own reactions are better if I'm relaxed, with the rod in rests. I've learned to place my rests so that I can pick up and strike in the one movement and, over the years, I've become fairly quick on the draw.

There *are* times when I find it necessary to hold the rod, but I don't do it with aching arms, tightly clenched fists and gritted teeth. I do it in a relaxed manner with the weight of the rod taken on a forward rod rest and my elbow on my knee. I feel for bites either on the index finger of the rod hand, or between the thumb and forefinger of the other.

Very often a chub will lie mouthing the bait without giving any real indication that it's doing so and this is sometimes followed by a rod-bending thump that results in precisely nothing, probably because it was caused by a sudden panic-stricken *rejection* of the bait rather than a confident bite.

There are dozens of different kinds of chub bites. You're likely to experience them all after winter floods have subsided, and there's no telling what they'll be like from one day to the next, but that shouldn't really bother you. I only worry when I get no bites at all!

Baffling Bream

'There are these enormous bream in the little river I fish back home,' said the fellow I was talking to in a North London tackle shop. 'They are knocking eight pounds, I'll swear,' he went on, 'but there's no way we can get near to catching them. Any ideas?'

This angler was talking about a Kentish water. A letter the same week from an angler in Norfolk had described an almost identical situation and asked virtually the same question. Earlier in the year the same question had been put to me at an anglers' forum in Hampshire, and I couldn't try to count the number of times I've been asked it over the past ten or fifteen years.

It's a problem I know well, and one which I've encountered on many different waters ever since I first began fishing. I don't know the answer because I don't believe there is one, but I do know that each situation is so very much like all the others that we might be talking about the same fish all the time.

In the past, with some luck, some thought and some preparation, I have managed to pick up a few of these bream from waters where I knew them to be difficult, but where I refused to admit that they were uncatchable. Not eight-pounders, but big fish for the water.

Big bream in small rivers interest me probably more than big bream in lakes, pits, and reservoirs, largely, I suppose, because they do not respond as well to logical thought or preconceived plans. I believe that, given time and patience, you can eventually catch big, stillwater bream by sheer persistence. You may not get the biggest of the shoal and you may not be able to hold the shoal long enough to catch more than one or two, but by sticking to and feeding one area continually, I believe you'll eventually be there when one of them makes a mistake. Sometimes one is enough. The satisfaction of seeing a single bream safely in the net after a long period of frustration is a just reward. Anything else that comes along is a bonus. I believe that's more or less how you have to look at the problem. To expect more than a modest success must lead to disappointment, and there will be more than a fair share of that anyway.

In theory, big bream in small rivers *ought* to be easier to catch than those in large, deep, enclosed waters. They should be easier to locate, and once located there should be very few problems involved in their capture. Bream are reputed to be fish with enormous appetites that suck up great carpets of groundbait and move on. But while this is possibly true of bream in many other situations, it's far from true of small river bream. Those, for some reason, are too often incredibly difficult.

They are, of course, wanderers. They have defined haunts where they may possibly be located at certain times, but it is at those times that they are most frustrating. They can be seen and, because they can be seen, they can be judged as to size and numbers, but at such times food of any kind does not interest them. One never knows for certain whether those fish are even present at other times. One wonders, when they can't be seen, whether they've moved out to feed elsewhere or whether they're lying deep, out of sight and just as uninterested in food as they were when they could be seen.

Occasionally, to add confusion, someone accidentally hooks a big bream, half a mile from where they were seen, while fishing for roach or dace with maggots or casters. It's an odd fish. Quite unexpected. The question then is whether or not it is one of the big shoal or an independent straggler. And one wonders whether the same kind of tactics might work in the spot the shoal is known to frequent.

Usually, of course, that spot is an incredible jungle of lily pads, bulrushes and other tackle-busting hazards and, even if successful fine-tackle techniques produce the bites, it's doubtful if the fish could be landed in the circumstances. Bream do not have a great reputation as fighters, but again, big bream in small rivers are different. They may not rip off yards of line but there's no stopping them on fine tackle.

The first shoal of big bream I ever spotted was on the River Thame, in a section of water where I'd learned to expect only small roach, small perch and the odd pike. I remember looking at them in utter disbelief, convinced that they averaged six pounds apiece. They probably averaged only half that weight, and in many years of fishing for them the best I ever caught weighed just over three and a half pounds.

I never caught more than one at a sitting but those bream took over my mind for about three seasons. I was young, inexperienced and unable to accept the fact that there was anything special about them other than their size. On reflection, those bream probably started me off on the tack known today as specimen hunting.

Those I caught were never taken as the result of any preconceived plan. They were there, I was a fisherman, and I kept pegging away in the hope that one day I'd be in the right place at the right time. I caught one on maggots, one on a little greyish worm, one on a piece of yellow paste, one on flour-and-water paste, referred to in those days as 'dough bait', and that's about all I can remember.

Opportunity to fish stopped shortly after that, and pollution later killed the bream off completely. But if they did nothing else for me, those fish helped me to recognise problems in later years.

The next shoal of small-river bream I found was on the upper Great Ouse.

We'd fished the water for years and caught good chub, roach, perch, dace and pike from it. We didn't then, and do not now, regard it as a bream water, but every so often news of a big bream being taken either upstream or downstream reached us. We never really knew whether to believe reports or not. They always reached us second hand and we never saw any proof of big bream's existence until we spotted a shoal of them ourselves in the swim we called 'the cabbage patch'. On and off we tried to catch them for about four years and then we decided to 'go for broke' one 16 June. It was an unusual venture, but it was worth trying, we thought.

All we did, in fact, was repeat more or less what we'd been doing for years for early-season tench. We removed the weeds and pre-baited. Our weed removal was different in that we had to cut lilies rather than drag out soft weed, but our pre-baiting was the same, though on a smaller scale. We used a multi-meal groundbait and a great heap of brandlings, and we took turns to bait the swim for, I think, two weeks in advance.

Previously we'd only fished by day, but we decided to start at midnight on this particular occasion. We'd estimated the biggest of those fish to be possibly seven pounds, but we were more than pleased to catch five of them weighing over five pounds apiece. That was one time, and the only one that I can remember, when a traditional approach proved successful for big bream in a small river.

Since then another big shoal has appeared but I've only ever caught one more fish, quite by accident, in a fining flood some years ago.

My friend and neighbour, Alan Brown, once latched into the second shoal and really went to town on them using single casters and very fine tackle. I'd told him where to find the fish. I knew they'd be around because I'd spotted them earlier, but I never rated his chance of catching them.

I also came very close to success once myself. If I'd not been so stupid I'd have caught some of the fish in the second shoal one winter's afternoon. I fished for them with a degree of optimism for some time but eventually quit and threw in all my spare bait, including a bait box of corn. Before I left the fishery I had the frustrating experience of watching those bream shovelling up my corn while I stood helpless, without bait of any kind, on the bank.

Today's improved float and loose-feeding techniques may possibly offer better chances of success with these difficult bream, but in the circumstances it's a long and difficult process. Unlike the big bream of the Thames these small river bream are not truly responsive. Finding them in feeding mood is as much a matter of luck as anything else, and you have to decide whether or not you can devote the time to them.

If you're the type of angler who refuses to admit that any fish is uncatchable, and if you're going to be satisfied with one fish (which is probably all you can hope for and which will almost certainly *not* be one of the biggest members of the shoal) then you'll enjoy the challenge. But if you're the kind of angler who likes to see fish in the net every trip, this will not really be a source of great pleasure.

Nevertheless, it's always worth remembering that being able to *see* the fish is at least proof of their existence. And every so often, in these circumstances, there comes a mad moment when the shoal decides to feed. You may just be there when it does. There's also a good chance, as I have proved with good-quality bream elsewhere, that a shoal will show all day, but begin to feed within half an hour of the sun going down.

They may well ignore any groundbait or loose feed put in front of them during the day, but every once in a while, when the sun has gone down, they'll up-end and scoop it all up within minutes. This often applies to still-water bream too, of course, but in the main I believe those are more predictable.

They were always regarded as summer fish at one time, but more and more good-quality bream are appearing in small rivers in winter these days. Perhaps our winters are milder, perhaps our bream have changed their habits. There was a time when I wouldn't have expected to see or catch bream in small rivers once October was here. Now nothing surprises me any more. But I'll go along with those who have spoken and written to me about catching the big ones. We'll never find them easy.

Light Relief

There's a great deal to be said for the occasional, light-hearted fishing session that involves no serious preparation and very little in the way of special bait. Throughout the summer months a great deal of our fishing time is spent during the early-morning or late-evening hours trying to catch fish that are often far from co-operative. Most of us agree, however, that the chances then are greater than during the day and we stick at it religiously until we achieve what we want—or until we suddenly realise we're no longer enjoying it.

This ceaseless quest for big fish, special fish, (every angler has a particular ambition, I'm sure) can be very wearing if results are not forthcoming. And it's then that a little light relief is called for. It's good for the morale if for nothing else to call a halt to these bloody-minded sessions and to go out and catch something easy—or at least easier.

It doesn't matter really what species are involved. What *is* important is that the fish are free biters and that they do not call for the dawn or dusk approach.

Recently my own light relief (and I welcomed it after a particularly unrewarding bream stint) came in the shape of a couple of dozen rudd. They were not big—the best weighed only eleven ounces, but they were *fun* to catch.

Rudd, of course, are not put off by warm water conditions as a rule, and carp anglers fishing with floating crust during the day regard them as out-and-out pests, but everything is relative in fishing. If you want carp on the bank you don't need rudd to distract you, but if you set out to catch the rudd on appropriate tackle it's a different cup of tea.

Rudd fishing can hold almost as much frustration at times as some of the more demanding kinds, but usually there's enough going on to keep you occupied. You can often see activity near the surface and that's enough to keep you pegging away.

You need tackle that isn't going to be too hard on small fish, but it has to be good casting tackle because, almost invariably, feeding rudd tend to drift further away from the bank with every cast you make.

I had my fun with a little wand of a rod, weighing under two ounces. My line was 2-pound test, and by using a heavy zoomer-type float I was able to get fair distance. This little 'Bo-peep' rod (my name for it incidentally, not a trade name) isn't designed for long casting. It's just a one-piece, five-foot, very soft-actioned stick that bends to the pull of a small fish, and I find it really alarming when something a bit bigger takes hold. But it's a rod I can use all day without fatigue and which gives me the maximum pleasure from small, easy fish.

A number of my friends laugh and say that it's quite impracticable, that there's no way you can control the line with a five-foot rod and that a much longer rod would be a more efficient tool. In many circumstances they'd be right, of course, but for long-distance shallow fishing for rudd, there's no advantage at all in a long rod. I would be casting, at times, in the region of forty yards, with my bait no more than a foot below the surface. Bites were slow, steady and determined and I could handle them perfectly well with the short rod. Had I been fishing deep, had the bites been mere flickers on the float, I'd probably have needed the extra sweep of a longer rod, but in this particular situation I was better off with the one I was using. Tucked under a tree as I was, I could not have executed a punch cast with a long rod without fouling the branches above, and these small rudd could never have given me so much sport.

It's a long time since I did any of this long-distance bank fishing for rudd. Most times I drift around for them in the boat, but I am reminded of earlier years when this kind of fishing was common practice. And I am very conscious of the fact that my modern floats are not a patch on those old ones I used fifteen or twenty years ago, which were dart-flight floats that cast well and remained visible at very long range. The thin vanes above the water line offered no resistance to biting fish but they stood out like brightly coloured 'bobbers' against the skyline. The thin-stemmed floats I used the other day were much more difficult to see.

There's still a lot to be said for some of the old ideas, and many of the rigs thought up years ago are still very practical today. I suppose the self-cocking float-cum-floating-crust-groundbait idea for rudd goes back for hundreds of years but it's still effective today if you can put it to work.

The Victorian anglers used to anchor their floating crust attractors in hairnets so that the rudd remained within casting range, and I've no doubt that the same idea would work today. As it is, most of us, myself included, tend to chuck out a few loose crusts for the rudd to locate, without paying too much attention to their line of drift. The usual result is that the fish eventually drift out of range with the crusts.

But, forgetting the effects of attractor crusts for a moment, it seems to me that, on some waters at least, rudd have a tendency to hug one particular line so far from the bank during the day. They may or may not be wise to anglers' bank shadows, but I've noticed that the better-quality rudd tend to stay well out until evening time. Casting directly to them, dropping a float in their midst, causes them to drift out even further, despite the fact that they'll take the hookbait the moment it lands. It's rather puzzling because this eagerness to take the bait surely proves that they're not actually scared by the tackle's entry. But you can almost be sure that the next cast you make will need another couple of feet added to it.

When I fished the other day I was fortunate in that the breeze was blowing across a wide corner and not out to the middle of the lake. It made the fishing a lot easier because, once the fish had drifted out past my maximum casting range from one bank spot, they just about came into range from the one opposite. Logically, the fish should have followed the loose crusts right into the margins where I could have fished for them under the rod tip, but they would only travel so far before taking up their original lies.

I spent a great deal of time moving from spot A to spot B in order to intercept them, and I didn't always succeed, but that's what made it all the more interesting. Here I had fish willing—even eager—to bite, and all I had to do was put the bait amongst them. Not quite as easy as it sounds but a good exercise nevertheless.

It gave me a pleasant afternoon's sport, a nice net of fish plus a few little problems; and it was a most welcome change from the flogging I'd been doing.

There are many other forms of what I call 'light-relief fishing' and I tend to practise them on and off throughout the season when the going's been tough.

I'll switch from barbel to dace for a time, or I'll leave the carp alone and fish up a storm with the comical little crucians. Sometimes I'll fish for eels during the heat of the day when the tench, bream or carp are off. And every so often I'll take the little 'Bo-peep' and flick out a little jig spinner for pike. I hope I never hook a big one on that outfit because even four-pounders feel like ocean-run monsters! But that's the whole point. I'm not out to break records or prove anything. I'm just seeking relief from a fishing that's become more of a chore than a pleasure.

I reckon everyone performs better after a break from monotony and I truly believe my light-relief fishing helps me handle the serious side a little better.

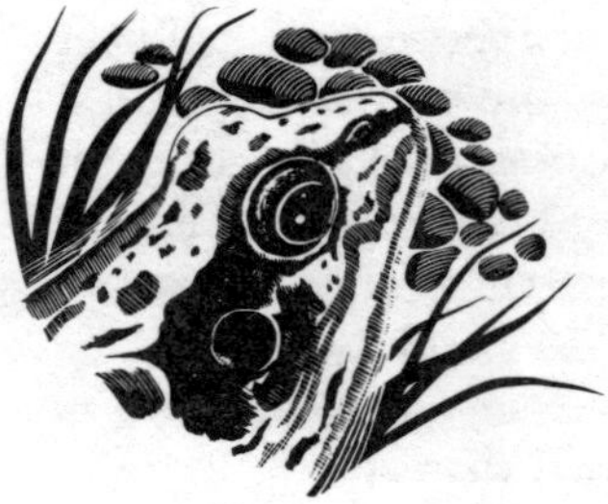

Unorthodox Tench

It is impossible to go through life as I have done, fishing whenever the opportunity arises and making the most of every spare minute at the water's edge, without encountering special days which suddenly make one sit up and say, 'By golly—I've *learned* something today.'

It has been said that every fishing trip teaches you something new, but I do not believe that this is strictly true. Sometimes the only thing I've learned on a fishing trip is that I was not as smart as I thought! And that's demoralising. But whatever your attitude towards fishing, whether you are a dabbler in the summer only, or a fanatic who fishes the year round, there are bound to be days when you learn something really worthwhile. The catch on that day may not be a spectacular one, but it will be remembered especially for the knowledge it brought.

I can recall many such days, and the first one that comes to my mind is a day I once spent as a boy in a boat at Halton Reservoir in Buckinghamshire.

I was roach fishing with two joints of a roach pole and a tight line. My father and uncle were tench fishing. They were using lobworms and paste baits 'laid on' with traditional tench tackle, and they had impressed upon me that I was not experienced enough to catch these fish.

My tackle was lighter; my bait was a grain of wheat fished well off the bottom below a light float. I caught lots of roach, but suddenly, as I was lifting out my tackle to re-cast, I found myself attached to something enormous. It was a tench, a big one, and of course I forgot everything I had been taught about letting the rod bend against the pull of the fish. I fairly heaved on the butt and the tench came thrashing across the top of the water to break the tackle long before I got it near the boat. That fish was a six-pounder according to the grown-ups who caught several five-pounders that day, and although I have lost count of the five-pounders I have since caught, I do not think I have ever hooked a bigger tench than that.

It was all very puzzling to a small boy. I was well tutored in the ways of fish and behaviour at the waterside by my father and uncles, who were fanatic fishermen in their day; they had told me that in order to catch tench it was essential to fish with big baits lying hard on the bottom—but my bait was a tiny wheat grain and it was not lying on the bottom.

They had further told me that it was important to wait for a bold run-away bite before striking at a tench. In fact, that was the way you told the difference between tench bites and bites from other fish. Yet my float had not moved at all. I don't suppose I realised it at the time, but that was when I began to wonder just how reliable the rule-of-thumb methods which had been handed down through the ages really were.

It took some time to sink in but it began to dawn on me, at quite an early age, that traditional tench fishing methods were not always one hundred per cent reliable. I could never forget that tench I hooked, and the memory of it was constantly nagging at me to try and apply the same technique for other tench. But it is difficult to change the thinking of generations of tench anglers when you're a small boy.

The trouble was that traditional tench methods worked often enough on most waters to discourage any change. Sooner or later, irrespective of depth, bait, tackle, etc., a tench would behave in the manner expected of it, and the half-cocked float would glide away forcefully when the big bait was taken. This added strength to what was probably false doctrine, for the truth is that time spent waiting for a textbook tench bite could well have been exploited in other ways, with the result that many more tench might have been caught.

I fished many tench waters in later years and some of them simply would not respond to orthodox bottom fishing as we know it. Traditional tench methods did not work there, and all the time remembering that the very first tench I ever hooked had behaved strangely, I was able to use other fishing methods and increase my catches.

I learned how to catch tench from the margins on very small baits fished so that they sank slowly between the reed stems. I was able to apply the lift method with its delicate bite registration when the tench were behaving in a manner which could only be described as finicky. I never thought up the lift method, nor, I am sure, was I the first to apply it to tench fishing, but I applied it to mine because I had learned long ago that tench do not always run off with a bait.

Today tench fishing proceeds along vastly different lines from those used before the Second World War, and my own tench fishing has changed a great deal because I realised so early in life that there was more to catching tench than chucking out a bait and waiting for a fish to hang on.

I learned that there were situations which demanded something different and that methods and baits had to be altered to suit each one.

I did not learn this all in the course of one day's tench fishing as a small boy, of course, but because of that early experience I began to *think* about my tench fishing. And I have always felt that if you think about any kind of fishing you're in with a better chance of success.

It is possible that all of this would have come to me a bit at a time later on even if I'd never had that disappointment early in my fishing life, but I believe that one experience has helped me to latch into hundreds of tench I would not normally have seen.

Deadly Corn

I caught my first tench on sweetcorn in 1949—on a hot July day, if I remember rightly—so there is nothing new about this 'modern bait'. (I referred to it in my first book *Angling in Earnest* as 'corn on the cob'.) It was not until years later that carp began to fall for it and for a time the great secrecy involved in its use (heaven knows why) brought confusion to the ranks of young anglers and beginners.

Forgetting, for the time being, about small boiled potatoes (a particle bait in effect) and other baits such as beans, peas, etc., all of which were tried when there were fewer carp and fewer carp anglers, and when the carp themselves responded well enough to paste, crust, flake and other regular baits, I recall my first introduction to serious carp fishing with particle baits. It was in 1967 in the USA that I first saw soaked corn used for carp, and let it be quite clear that corn, and the varieties of it that may or may not be available here, is cob corn and not wheat.

The soaked corn I saw used in the USA was field corn. It grows exactly like sweetcorn. It is, however, used, as far as I know, exclusively for meal and flour and is not eaten on the cob. It is not sweet like sweetcorn; it is harvested around November and the very hard grains are threshed out. Sweetcorn, often eaten on the cob, is indeed, as the name suggests, sweeter. It is harvested while still soft and milky around July or August and is cooked on the cob, and, of course, can be grown and purchased in Britain. Whether or not the American field corn is obtainable here I do not know, but the nearest thing to it that I know is the grain known generally as Indian maize. Whether it comes from India or not I have no idea. It is not bright yellow like the American corn I have seen, but rather a dull reddish colour, and is, if anything, much harder.

In the absence of the one, however, I tried the other, soaking it for weeks on end in the way the Americans do, and I learned immediately that it had great attractive powers. The smell of the fermenting maize is exactly the same as the smell of fermenting American field corn, and it remains just as immune to the attentions of small fish.

Carp can manage it without difficulty and they'll eat it in great quantities. The fact that it never really softens doesn't seem to put them off. So, for general purposes, ordinary maize in its full-grain state, the kind that can be bought fairly reasonably by the sack or bushel from any corn merchant, can be soaked, allowed to ferment and develop its own peculiar attractive smell, and may be used as groundbait and hookbait for our carp. It is also effective for bream and tench as I have proved many times.

Maize has one drawback, however, in that it often results in lost fish, presumably because of its hardness. It will blunt a sharp hook to such an extent that it needs to be re-sharpened after baiting, and even then the strike is often impeded when more than one grain is used. A much better hookbait is sweetcorn which can be purchased from any supermarket either frozen or in cans. In season, of course, it can be bought absolutely fresh and can be used straight from the cob, as can the deep-frozen variety. Tinned sweetcorn needs no preparing, either: it can be used straight from the tin.

Sweetcorn (which I emphasise again as being softer, sweeter, and needing no cooking or soaking, generally speaking) is, on the other hand, a lot more expensive than maize, and if it is to be used in any quantity the best buy is the six-pound catering size tin. It is excellent as both hookbait and groundbait, and is a much better hooker than hard maize; but there is no way, in my opinion, that it will ever have the attractiveness that American corn or Indian maize seem to have for fish. I'm no great believer in essences and scents as bait additives, but there is no possible doubt in my mind that the deadliness of soaked American corn or soaked Indian maize lies in its smell.

I have, of course, combined both maize and sweetcorn in an attempt to get the best out of both worlds and I am inclined to believe, after a number of sessions, that tinned sweetcorn, emptied into a container of fermenting maize so as to soak up the same flavour, is superior to that used fresh from the tin.

It is worth mentioning here, perhaps, that stewing maize, or placing it in a thermos of boiling water to swell like wheat, does not really soften it. Nor does it make it in any way more attractive to the fish.

I think it is also worth mentioning that it takes several days' soaking to develop the right kind of smell, and that from then on it tends to become progressively stronger, which, as far as I can see, is an advantage.

It is a bit anti-social, however, unless you've a completely covered container to soak it in, and a long garden in which to leave it to mature. But do *not* leave it in soak in a vessel with a tight-fitting or screw-on lid! The pressure that builds up while maize ferments has to be seen to be believed, and the explosions that sometimes occur (usually covering someone with an evil liquid that smells like a brewery gone wrong) can be dangerous. By all means keep a lid on it, but ease it up occasionally in case it becomes stuck.

Having started off a baiting session with soaked maize, and having kept it up for a few days, it is not strictly necessary to continue along the same lines. From then on it is enough to take the dry maize straight from the sack and introduce it as it is. It will soak naturally in the water, and give off (one assumes) the same flavour as the initial offerings. It then becomes one of the most convenient baits possible to acquire. It keeps virtually for ever, needs no refrigeration or protection from cold, and, generally speaking, is a clean bait to handle.

Operation Re-launch

I finally made it! I got out into a swim at Wotton Lakes in the big old pontoon with the canopy intact, the bottom bone dry and a few tench in the swim.

It had taken a long time. The last trip in that boat had been way back in 1972 (I think) when my young friend Malcolm Baldwin had caught a twenty-pound pike on a cold winter's day. It was then that we discovered that the bottom was rotten, likely to fall to pieces at any moment and, although it didn't belong to us, Ken and I decided we'd talk the owner, John Mason, into hauling it out, and try to repair it. At first it was going to be a patch here and a patch there but we quickly discovered that there was no way we could mend it. The whole bottom had to be knocked out, and so we started knocking. John went pale when he saw what we were doing and I know that he mentally wrote the whole thing off there and then.

But the structure was sound, the two big oak runners at the base were still solid, and we decided that, if we could get it all really dry, we could restore the boat completely. The pontoons are about twenty feet long, six feet wide and weigh a couple of tons so it was a big task. But luck was with us. The summer of 1973 was hot and dry, and we were able to start rebuilding in the autumn. We soaked any suspect areas with bitumen and/or creosote and killed off all signs of fungus (there had been plenty), re-boarded the bottom with rough timber, nailed directly to the original oak runners, and over a long period covered the whole bottom and part of the sides with heavy gauge aluminium sheet.

We swamped the inside with bitumen, sealed the joins in the aluminium with fibreglass and covered them with a foil-backed adhesive bitumen sheet. I don't know how many shirts and pairs of trousers I ruined slopping gallons of black paint around, and I've never really added up what we all paid out to restore the old girl, but with fitted floorboards, deck chairs, folding canopy, mooring-pole clamps, anchors, rod-rest fixings and a lot of other extras we consider it was well worth all the work and expense involved.

It was like old times again when I paddled her out to a shallow, mud-bottomed swim no more than three feet deep, and baited up overnight with John and Ken. It had been a poor start to the season by all accounts, but as I had not been in the country at the time I had not been in a position to see for myself. There had been plenty of tench activity but very little in the way of tench bites, and if some of my serious tench-fishing friends couldn't catch them I'm quite sure I'd have failed too. So, perhaps, I didn't miss much through being away.

I must have timed my return to coincide with a general improvement in the tench fishing and I had a feeling that, even though I'd had no time to prepare a swim or to pre-bait it over a period, I'd chosen right. I couldn't tell you why, but I felt sure that I'd get a few tench next morning. The only points I'd considered were the mud bottom, the depth and the fact that the swim was surrounded by soft silkweed. There was no weed at all where John and I tipped in the brandlings, stale bread, and other oddments in our rather hurried overnight baiting session, but we spent a bit of time turning over the mud with long paddles and giving it a general murky hue before we left.

I won't say the next morning's fishing was perfect, indeed, if the truth be told, it must have been boring for Ken and John who caught nothing at all, but at least there were tench feeding in the swim, and I had four in the region of four pounds-plus before we left in the middle of the morning.

That's nothing to crow about, of course, and the fact that the only four fish caught came to my rod in no way suggests that I did anything different or better than the other two. That part of it was luck and nothing more, but I felt pleased about the swim generally.

Big lobs were the baits the tench preferred and they took them very, very slowly, cautiously and with a great deal of preliminary twitching and sucking, all of which didn't help because we all missed fish through being impatient.

My first indication of tench being present came when I hooked and lost a fish early on. I had thought it was a pike because of its great power, but there was a great wodge of tench slime on the hook-line to prove me wrong. Ken and I have always had a little 'thing' about tench slime. We never remove it from the line but push it up so that it hangs around the cocking shot or shots because we half-believe it helps attract other tench. It was all said with a great deal of false confidence of course but both Ken and I told John that the first fish would come to my rod because of the tench slime on my line. And it did. So did the next one, and each time I added a bit more to the slime around my shot.

John didn't know whether to believe us or not, and Ken made a great pretence of pleading with me for 'just a small piece', but I was feeling mean that day and refused.

At one stage I caught him trying to steal some while I was putting a fish in the keepnet and I reckon that's about as sneaky as you can get! But it did him no good whatsoever—he missed the next bite completely.

A couple of friends fished the same swim at my suggestion during the next day or two. They caught a few fish themselves and, of course, kept the swim baited during that period. I believe it is better to share a swim in this fashion than to try and keep it a secret. A swim worked on will often continue to produce; one left alone for several days may end up by being vacated.

John Ingham and I fished there the following day. We started at eleven a.m. and left around six-thirty p.m. We *ought* to have caught a lot of tench, but in fact we shared a bag of ten averaging four pounds. We were both ashamed of the number we missed and lost, but it did seem to us that the tench were simply hanging on to the very end of the lob before swimming off with it. Very few of them took the whole worm confidently, and there were no bites at all on smaller pieces or other baits.

Not that it mattered very much. We had fished at the worst possible time and still caught some nice fish, which is all we'd hoped for. Next time, perhaps, we'll start earlier and catch them in a confident mood, but I'm not too worried.

What's important to me is to have fish in the swim. If I can't catch them then it's my own fault. And anyway I enjoy fishing off the old pontoon even if I don't catch anything at all.

Untypical Roach

I've always said that my favourite kind of fishing is the one I happen to be doing at the time, but that if I had to be restricted to one species of fish I'd choose roach every time (on this side of the Atlantic, at least). There's no room for the words 'always' and 'never' in the world of angling (as has been said many times by those more informed than I), but I believe it's fairly safe to say that you can never be sure about roach and that there are so many different situations that you can always reckon on surprises one way or the other.

In recent years my roach fishing has not been up to scratch because many of the waters I fish have been short of quality fish. Indeed, some of them seemed to be completely devoid of roach. But now there are signs of improvement, and recent experiences have led me to believe that there's a chance of getting back to normal. I have been pleasantly surprised by my catches, not because the weights were outstanding or made up of big fish but rather because a few better-than-expected fish put in an appearance.

On one occasion I was fishing for tench with sweetcorn in one of the better-known swims on a Lincolnshire lake. It was late afternoon and while there were no signs to encourage me whatsoever, I wasn't unduly bothered. It was not a serious venture, merely an escape for a couple of hours, and I was in no mood for hard and serious concentration. It was a simple case of sitting under a tree with a couldn't-care-less attitude. If something decided to hang on at its end of the line I'd hang on at mine. As simple as that. And sometimes that's the right attitude to take. If you're not really bothered, a few fish help to improve the hour. If you're out for blood, failure to catch fish is depressing, and if you've built up your hopes too high and things don't work out, you find yourself trying to figure out why.

There's nothing wrong with that approach, of course. It's really the only way to overall success, but there *are* times when it gets you all screwed up and wondering. Sometimes it's better to treat fishing as an excuse to do nothing! That's how it was with me that day.

All the more pleasant, then, was it to see the small antenna float disappear slowly and positively, and a roach of about three-quarters of a pound come sliding to the net. I knew that roach had shown occasionally here and there in the lake after several years of apparent absence, and I'd caught several in the quarter-pound bracket on maggots and casters before, but I'd not seen a half-pounder for some time. I was astonished, therefore, to catch another five, including one of about one and a quarter pounds. The best I've caught from that water in over twenty years as far as I can remember.

In my eagerness, I suppose I spoiled my own chances by trying to hold the shoal with extra feed. I know that sweetcorn is very filling and that it's all too easy to over-feed, but I'm fairly sure that's what happened. I've done it before with stewed wheat, and I ought to have known better, but when bites slow down or stop, it becomes almost automatic to try and restart the process. But once you've over-fed a swim, that's it. The damage is done; you can't undo it.

But at least it was encouraging to know that the roach were back again. Later in the year (if I could find them), I told myself, they would be in even better condition and if sweetcorn remained as acceptable to them there would be a great opportunity to fish for them without being plagued by hordes of tiny rudd.

There's a lot still to be said for the so-called old-fashioned big-baits-for-big-fish approach. It doesn't always work; and you should never rely upon it to work, but in many situations it still applies. I have even known it apply to a number of heavily fished maggot/caster/hempseed waters, and I am still of the opinion that you can often catch better-quality fish from these waters whilst at the same time avoiding the small unwanteds.

My local carp water teems with tiny roach and rudd. They are always hungry, always troublesome unless you really want to catch them for live or deadbaits. Then, of course, they're a god-send. Otherwise, nothing is sacred to them and even the biggest crust or flake hookbait is torn to shreds in seconds. Potatoes, maize, beans and other accepted carp baits, however, are immune from their attentions.

This is a typical carp-fishing situation; a situation where the busy-busy activity of thousands of small fish can be used to attract carp or start them off feeding—even in winter.

With these thoughts in mind, and with hopes of one more carp before winter, I sat one sunny afternoon through with a free-line tackle and a No. 10 hook baited with a fair-sized knob of very stiff paste. I figured the carp would be more inclined to take a 'cherry' than a 'golf ball' at the tail-end of summer, and I hoped the tight texture of the bait would deter the small fry. It did, to a certain extent.

There were whittlings and knockings and twitches on the line, all of which would have caused a regular float tackle to have 'misbehaved', but which could not seriously affect a floatless rig. I reckon it took about five minutes for each piece of bait to succumb and I knew at once when the hook was bare because all movement ceased immediately. It is a perfectly normal occurrence; one which I've learned to accept philosophically in the knowledge that there can be no mistaking the carp run when it comes. A traditional, old-fashioned and still very reliable way of catching carp in many waters.

My run came after about an hour and I struck in time to prevent the carp from taking the tackle into the rush-bed nearby. Carp? I'd hoped it would be, indeed I'd never considered anything else. But I was to be surprised. A roach of about a pound gave up the ghost very quickly on the end of the 7-pound line and I lifted it ashore. (Many years ago, I had taken rudd up to just over two pounds from that water, but in all the years I had fished there I had never seen a roach weighing a pound. It would normally take about thirty to make up that weight!)

There wasn't much pleasure involved. That kind of tackle can hardly be regarded as suitable for roach and I'd have preferred to catch the fish on something a lot more delicate, but I had to consider the possibility of a biggish carp. By the end of the day, I had eight roach in all, all bigger than I'd ever seen before from that water, but none bigger than the first.

As it happens, I didn't get my carp and, on reflection, I might have improved my roach chances had I scaled down immediately. I would almost certainly have enjoyed the actual catching of those roach more had I been less heavily tackled. But I wonder if I'd have even *seen* those roach in different circumstances? Perhaps they were some old diehards that had avoided capture until then, but they looked remarkably fine fish to me and it gave me real pleasure to know they were there.

A little clear stream, where the roach grow fairly big and appear to know very well what is and what is not attached to a hook, was the scene of my third experience.

Here there is no question of fishing blindly. You simply apply stealth and caution until you spot a shoal of fish, then drive yourself completely out of your mind trying to catch them! You sit there and flick in the odd few maggots or casters and you watch them ignore them all. You don't even think about using tackle at this stage. If you do, you might as well go home and have done with it.

It's a long process, but after a time one of the fish begins to take an interest in the loose feed and eventually it sucks in a maggot—and spits it out again at once. That's about the time you begin to think you *might* be making progress. But still you do *not* touch the rod. You feed sparingly but regularly and watch what happens. Presently the same roach sucks in a maggot and does *not* spit it out. More progress. Soon it is taking confidently, and the very fact that it is doing so seems to serve as a stimulant to the other members of the shoal. Soon they are all feeding.

That's real progress. Now you have to settle in some distance above them and feed at a rate which holds them where they are. Then, and only then, is it advisable to send the hookbait down. It's not easy. In fact it is one of the most difficult forms of fishing I have ever practised—one mistake and it's all over. It's seldom possible to reassure those fish into feeding again.

I don't have to tell you that the tackle has to be gossamer, that the bait has to behave as nearly as possible like an unattached portion, or that the tackle must not be dragged back directly through the swim but drawn back slowly on a different line. These are the simple clear-water, roach-fishing facts of life. But if everything goes as planned you can then hope to get bites and catch fish.

I did all of that on that occasion, and although I'm sure I followed the right procedure down to the smallest detail, I could not get a bite.

In fact, I was able, from a concealed spot, to watch the roach taking every maggot coming through *except* the one on the hook. Obviously my presentation was at fault, but I could not improve it in any way with the tackle I had available.

In the end I gave up, but, just to be stubborn, I put up some heavier gear, stuck a big knob of paste on a No. 10 hook, eased it down, and let it lie on the bottom. Nothing. I began drawing back slowly for another cast and, while the bait was proceeding upstream, spinning like a top in the current, a roach of 1 pound 9 ounces nailed it. Three more fish did exactly the same thing, and at this stage I began to ask myself, 'What's all this about presentation then?'

As I said earlier, you can *never* be sure about roach fishing, and it is the element of surprise that makes it all the more absorbing.

Combined Operation

The little Berkshire stream had been well and truly over its banks as the great tide-line of dead reeds, branches, soft weed and debris halfway across the meadow clearly indicated. Even now it was above normal winter level, but the water had fined down and I could see the bottom in all but the deepest spots.

Throughout the summer, the roach, dace, and occasional chub of this little river are widely distributed in small groups that could hardly be called shoals, and compiling anything like a bag of fish means you have to travel with as little gear as possible, extracting a fish here and another there by using roving techniques. It always seems a pleasant form of fishing to me, not having to hump around loads of groundbait and extra tackle. A made-up rod, some bits and pieces of bait and a landing net (just in case) are the only real necessities.

Later in the year, after the first flush-through, the fish usually shoal up more and tend to inhabit the deeper water, leaving most of the rest of the river fishless. The previous season, as I recall, we had no flood, and it was not until the tail end that the fish showed signs of shoaling. Most of the time it was hardly worthwhile settling in one spot and fishing. This year the flood came early.

It undoubtedly set the little river off to a fine start, and some of the shoals would almost certainly stay put from then until the end of the season. Ken and I were impressed with the condition of the water and, hopefully, began to fish for the roach we knew to be there.

First trot down, and without any preliminary feeding, I hooked a big roach. Big by my standards, anyway; I estimated it at around a pound. It came off at the net, unfortunately, and from that moment on I could only catch dace in that spot. It was a busy little swim that produced a bite every run-through, and though I missed plenty I did reasonably well.

They were fine fish, but I am not a dace fanatic. I cannot work up any enthusiasm for traditional floatfishing for dace. Catching them by other methods intrigues me, especially if I can *see* the fish and induce them to take right on the surface either on bait or fly, but I soon tire of continual trotting when I know the next fish is going to be the same as the last.

Two small chub around the three-quarter-pound mark (and which I first thought were above-average dace) held my attention for a little longer, but after a time I moved on in search of roach. I met Ken, who had had a similar experience and who had the same thoughts in mind. Here and there we spotted roach in the clear water, but they were not shoaled, as we had hoped they would be. An odd pair here, three or four mixed up with a small dace shoal, and one lone big fish which we scared, were all we could locate. None of them warranted serious fishing in their present surroundings and further efforts in the deeper corners again resulted in dace, many of which were small, but from which we selected a dozen deadbaits for pike fishing later.

It was midday when we spotted the big roach. There were only half a dozen, but, of those, three would have undoubtedly topped the two-pound mark. They were lying tucked under a big alder, completely inaccessible and as safe as an office block. There was no way I could see of tackling them, but at least the protection of the tree covered our movements too and we were able to watch.

Their dark shapes were hardly visible for most of the time, but every few minutes they would drop back and show briefly.

What followed was the most interesting yet frustrating experience I have enjoyed for seasons.

For some reason those fish simply would not react to loose feeding from above. I watched the maggots Ken tossed in upstream come trickling through the branches trailing in the water, and I actually saw some of them bounce off the noses of the fish as they headed into the current.

I decided there and then that they were definitely not going to feed. It's an old dodge, of course, in these circumstances, to try and make the fish react one way or the other depending upon the amount of feed used. You don't expect them to start feeding at once, but you can sometimes either draw them upstream out of their haunt, or cause them to drop back. It's not necessarily a feeding reaction—merely one of curiosity—but very occasionally it is a preliminary to a feeding pattern. And the object, of course, is to draw them out of their hidey-hole *before* they start to feed. Those roach would have none of it!

'I'll try flicking in some bread so that it sinks right in among them,' said Ken. I shrugged and said he might as well try, but somehow I couldn't imagine those roach would be interested in bread, having ignored maggots and casters for the last hour. Which just goes to show how wrong you can be.

The first few pieces Ken dropped in were ignored, but a few seconds later the roach dropped back very slowly and began to take each piece quite determinedly. I never cease to be excited about actually watching fish feed; to me it's as absorbing as the fishing itself. But there was still no way that I could see of putting a float tackle among those roach. I tried, but it was quite hopeless.

Ken suggested that I might be able to do something without the float. After all, he pointed out, there was no need for bite registration other than the sight of the bait being taken! He was right, of course.

I took the float off, pinched a small piece of flake on to the hook, flicked it downstream, and drew it up carefully so that it hung in the current above the fish, about six inches below the surface and out of their immediate vision.

Then, as Ken continued to feed and the roach continued to take, I tried to release the slack line so that my hookbait sank on approximately the same plane. There was absolutely no doubt about it: those roach knew that something wasn't right.

They took all the loose pieces, but would have nothing to do with the one on the hook. It was a perfect example of bait presentation, or to be more precise, bad presentation. The hookbait hung in the current wrongly, and my attempts to steer it, by rod-tip manipulation, into their line of vision simply made them suspicious.

Eventually, I scaled the tackle right down, pinched a tiny piece of bread on to the hook point, slid the single shot a yard up the line and, holding some slack in my hand, waited for an opportunity. Ken, at my suggestion, tossed in half a dozen slightly larger pieces of bread, and simultaneously, I let the hook bait sink by releasing the slack line.

The shot took it down quickly so far, and then it began to sink naturally in the current. It disappeared into the mouth of one of the roach and I struck the only way possible—by snatching the line in my left hand. I could not raise the rod. It was poked between the branches of the tree, but I managed to keep it low, draw it out and coax the fish into open water before landing it. I'd like to say it was the biggest of the shoal, but in fact it was one of the smallest. It might *just* have weighed a pound, but it was probably an ounce under. We didn't weigh it and it was such a bonny fish that we put it back immediately upstream of the action.

It took the remaining fish half an hour to show again and we eventually caught another, almost identical, by the same strategy.

Those two fish would have meant nothing much had they been part of a bag of lesser fish or if they'd been taken by traditional methods, but in the circumstances they provided a couple of hours of great interest for two anglers. I think both Ken and I learned something, and although we failed to achieve any real results, at least we think we *might* possibly be able to select and catch a two-pounder one day. The chances are, of course, that we shall never see those roach again, but it's always pleasant to hope. Two-pound roach have been very few and far between for both of us, and future possibilities are intriguing.

Two questions come to my mind at once regarding the fish we

caught. Why were they so interested in bread when they showed no signs of even recognising maggots? Why did they take those tiny pieces of bread, balanced as they were on the very point of the No. 12 hook with the rest of it clearly visible? (I left the No. 12 on because I anticipated having to use a fair amount of pressure in order to pull the hooked fish out of trouble, but I was prepared, if necessary, to go a lot smaller.)

And I wonder how I would have felt had I succeeded in catching a personal best roach by those tactics? It was a joint effort. I have only one pair of hands and there is no way I could have dealt with the situation without Ken's constant help.

As it happened, there was no need for concern; the fish we caught were of no great importance. But what if there had been a record involved? Who could have claimed it?

It Happened One Night

Fifteen or sixteen years ago, like a good many others at the time, I was stricken by the carp-fishing bug. Carp were the 'in' fish! I had my Mark IV rods and my electric bite-alarms, and I felt quite sure that the opportunity to fish a good carp water was all I needed to prove that I too, could catch big carp.

Well, it all depends upon what you call big, of course. I reckoned anything over ten pounds would do; I never kidded myself that anything under twenty pounds was small-fry as some folk still tend to do.

The opportunity came, and with it a few carp and an increased knowledge of how carp tend to behave. It didn't all come at once, but I became what I now consider to be a fairly competent carp fisher.

I stuck with one water because I believed then, as I do now, that it pays to learn one water properly and not flit from one to the other in the mistaken belief that the grass is greener elsewhere. The more I fished that one water, the more I learned of its occupants and their moods.

I also learned how to handle a big fish in the darkness; but there was one memorable day which, though it brought me no reward in the shape of fish, taught me two lessons I have never forgotten.

Perhaps I should say 'memorable night', for it all happened in darkness.

I have always believed in making myself very familiar with any tackle I am going to use at night and, for this reason, if two fishing outfits are likely to be used either separately or at the same time I make sure that they are identical. On this occasion I had two Mark IV outfits similarly rigged with lines, reels and hooks. I knew that whichever one I picked up would feel the same in my hands after dark. I knew only too well that, in the past, every time I had chosen to use a strange reel at night, the only bites I had had were on that outfit. It was always so.

But on this occasion I had familiarised myself with the tackle and I had been very careful about the reel clutch. It was set to slip nicely well below the pull needed to break my 9-pound line, and I was very well satisfied that I had done everything I could to ensure success.

I had fished all through the previous night and all that day as well. Now I was tired, but quite confident that I could stay awake for the second night as well.

I suppose it was about two o'clock in the morning when I was awakened by my bite-alarm. Yes, I'd fallen asleep very quickly despite my cockiness, and, like a good many others, I was literally caught napping.

I grabbed the rod and struck, remembering instinctively to snap home the bale arm at the same time. I have no way of knowing for certain, but I was quite sure at the time that the fish I hooked was much bigger than I had caught earlier. It hared across towards the other side of the lake and the rod was pulled mercilessly down towards the water. I could not raise it and, within seconds, the fish, line and rod were all pointed in the same direction and the line snapped.

Theoretically, the clutch should have slipped long before this could have happened, but it didn't, and when I tested it afterwards I found it to be quite tight. I know I had not readjusted it—it had tightened up of its own accord in the cold night air.

Several other carp anglers of my acquaintance reported similar happenings later, and we were generally agreed that a particularly cold night can sometimes affect the delicate clutch setting of a fixed-spool reel. I do not know the real reason for it. Possibly grease inside the reel, which has softened in the sun, becomes hard again when the temperature drops. At one time I thought that it might perhaps have been due to the contraction of some metal part when the night became cold, but I am not sure.

What I *am* sure about is that it pays to allow for such happenings and set the clutch a little lighter than at first appears necessary. And it is advisable to check several times throughout the night as well. Or set it really slack at the outset—which is probably the best procedure.

In those early carp-fishing days I became excited whenever I had a run at night and I could never remember to put my finger on the spool when I struck. So for that reason, I never fished with a really loose clutch setting. Today, I am older, wiser and less inclined to become hysterical. Today, I remember things I used to forget. Like the fact that you can't stay awake for ever, for instance!

Had I kept my wits about me that night and not been half stupid with sleep, it would have been quite a simple matter for me to have adjusted that reel clutch quickly in the few seconds before the line snapped. But I thought I was smart and didn't want to lose a minute of my precious carp-fishing time.

Well, it's happened to better anglers than me and I expect it will happen again, but such things happen to me only once! I don't let them happen again. I try hard to convince anglers, particularly young anglers, that you need to be at your best when you've got a big carp on at night. I know that if you try to go for too long without sleep you will be unable to meet the situation when that little bit extra is called for.

I've never forgotten that carp I lost and to the best of my knowledge I have never hooked a bigger one since. I doubt if I ever shall now, but although the disappointment is still with me, it is more than made up for by the lessons I learned that night. Lessons learned the hard way are all part of the serious business of becoming a fisherman.

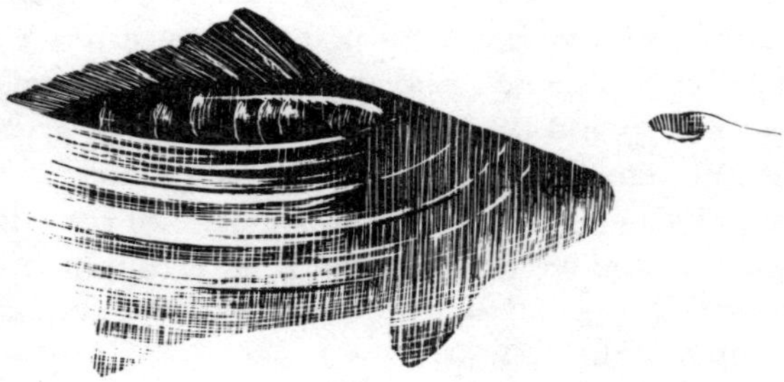

Learning Lessons

I suppose there are plenty of times when match anglers go home feeling pretty fed-up with the way they've fished on a certain day, and it's been my experience that the best of them make no bones about it. Far from making excuses for their bad results by blaming conditions or any one of a hundred other factors, most of them have said, 'I fished like an amateur and it was my own fault.' Or, 'I could have won it hands down if I'd used my loaf.' Which makes me believe that I'm not the only one who has had bad days more often than is desirable. And that's a consolation.

But do matchmen have spells when everything seems to go wrong; or do they learn by their mistakes and put things right next trip? If they do they're either fortunate or smarter than I am, for it seems I've been doing a lot of things wrong recently without learning too much from my experiences. Which is bad. And, I've had more than my share of mishaps, too, over which I seem to have had no control at all.

After losing three carp in one night because I'd put the bait in a spot where the bite had to be hit immediately and not left to develop into a regular run, you'd think I could have organised things better the following night. But I was pig-headed enough to think I'd just been unlucky and that if I fished the same style in the same place again I'd eventually tie into a carp that stayed with me. It didn't happen that way, of course. I lost two more.

I figured it out that the chances of a bite were greater off the edge of the rush-bed than anywhere else and that it was better to fish there and take a chance than to fish well away from it and not get a bite. What happened was that the comparative novice I had with me fished where I'd decided *not* to fish, had two good runs, hooked two carp and landed them both.

I was more than pleased for him, but I was angry with myself for fishing like a clown. The loss of a couple of carp didn't mean much, but it would have been better if we'd caught all four. That would have been a good night, even though the carp would have averaged only eight pounds.

You never know what to do for the best, of course, but I should have learned by the mistakes I had made previously.

I've always figured that I could put things together reasonably well and when I missed a whole batch of tench bites on full lobs, I felt pretty sure that the tench were just taking hold of the tail end and running off. On many other occasions the answer to this particular problem has been to use tail ends only, so naturally that's what I did. I didn't get a bite, whereas my companion, fishing the same swim with whole lobs, caught four averaging four pounds apiece. Halfway through the session I almost changed over to whole lobs myself but I was too stubborn for my own good and the result was a fair one. Served me right!

I fished Damerham Lakes for trout soon afterwards and a friend, who knows the water much better than I, suggested that I'd be better off with a brown or green fly line instead of the white one I was using. But I liked the white line because I could see it better at the point where the leader joins, so I stuck with it all day. Result? My friend had eight trout and I had only one! Again—it served me right.

I *did* learn from this experience, however, and I dyed the darn thing bottle-green immediately I arrived home. On the next trip, in similar conditions, I caught a limit including a nice fish of 5 pounds 6 ounces. Perhaps, I thought, my luck is changing. The green line might help me catch fish more easily on the river, and, in fact, I think it did.

I had my limit quicker, at any rate, but I'm not too sure whether it was luck, better fishing on my part, or the fact that I'd been using a different line. I did notice, however, that I seemed to *scare* fewer fish than usual.

So, from the actual fishing point of view, I suppose I learned from my mistakes but I failed miserably to learn about other things. In the boot of my car there is *always* a change of clothing just in case of emergencies, but when I travelled in Ken's car two weeks ago I didn't bother to take them. And you might as well know I fell in that cold chalkstream halfway through the morning!

As I struggled out, I consoled myself with the thought that I'd have dry clothes at the car, and it wasn't until I'd squelched my way back that I remembered it wasn't my car I was heading for. It's definitely *not* comfortable trying to fish in oilskin over-trousers and nothing else.

Last week, naturally, I took the spare clothing, but for some reason I forgot my gumboots. And at six a.m. it's not very pleasant walking through long grass after heavy rain in carpet slippers, which is what I always wear for driving. Ken, however, had a brainwave. 'Plastic bags,' he said. 'There's a whole bunch in the boot. Put 'em on over your socks, hold 'em up with rubber bands, and wear your over-trousers and slippers on top.'

It was a great idea, and while I doubt very much if it's original, it did work and is worth remembering. A few plastic bags, or better still a length of lay-flat plastic tubing, will take up no room and will always serve for an emergency such as this. My feet stayed dry and later, when the sun dried out the grass, I was able to dispense with the bags and carry on as usual.

A little later I was bragging about the idea to the keeper. 'Look at that,' I said. 'Bone-dry despite the weather and wet grass earlier.'

He was suitably impressed. Later he called me over to the shade of a big tree that sloped over the water and pointed out a big trout under the far bank.

'If you can balance yourself on the tree trunk,' he said, 'and flick your fly just above it, you might be in business.' He didn't wait to see the end result but went about his duties.

Ken watched from a distance for a moment or two and then wandered off downstream in search of another fish, while I concentrated on the one I could see. The soles of my slippers, however, had by now developed a sheen and the greasy bark of the tree trunk made the situation a precarious one, to say the least.

Ken heard the splash and called, 'Are you in?' Meaning, of course, 'Are you into a fish?'

'Yes,' I spluttered. 'I'm in all right—up to the waist!'

The fish disappeared rapidly, but I confess to a little smirk of satisfaction when I caught it an hour later—this time in my bare feet. I travelled home in dry clothes and though I was picking bits of thistle from my feet for some time afterwards, I suppose it worked out fairly well all round. But I doubt if I'll forget my wellies again! Perhaps that's one lesson I'll remember for the future, but with the way my luck's been going recently, I'm prepared for anything.

There's a big wasp's nest in my rock garden and I was discussing with my wife the possibility of getting out the cake for bait. 'I'll cyanide it,' I said. 'Or else I'll burn it out with petrol and then dig it out.'

'I shouldn't bother if I were you,' she said sweetly. 'The way your luck is at present you'll either poison yourself, blow yourself up or get stung to death!'

Perhaps she's right. Anyone want some wasp grubs?

The Beanfeast

Every so often there comes a day, or a night, which you as an angler know you're going to remember for a long time. I don't necessarily mean the times when you catch big fish or big bags of fish, but times when things happen to make you remember and think about what happened.

Sometimes they're things that go wrong, sometimes things that go right, but they end up as talking points for a long time afterwards. And that's half what fishing's all about, anyway.

Take the other night, for instance. I felt that time was getting on a bit and that I ought to go out and make the effort to catch at least one more carp before the summer season ended.

Our carp don't run big locally. There are a few double-figure fish, but they're mostly around the eight-pound mark, which is quite enough to give you a lot of fun in a confined space after dark. Hook one of those under your rod point and it's all-get-out for a few moments, I can tell you. Never mind about twenty- or thirty-pounders. Carp are carp, and, while I admit that the bigger they come the better I like it, I am never, I promise you, going to despise, or become blasé about, seven- or eight-pounders. I've had quite enough of them come adrift from time to time to know that they deserve respect.

At one time I felt that a carp weighing much less than twelve pounds wasn't worth having. Very big-headed I was in those days, and quite certain that twenty- and thirty-pounders would come my way as a matter of course.

In fact they never did, and although I've caught a great many ten-pound-plus fish I've never caught a twenty-pounder yet. I doubt very much now if I ever will because I'm not quite so dedicated a carp angler as I used to be and I no longer fish waters that I know to hold twenty-pounders. My fishing time seems to get less and less and I have to try and take advantage of what I have. I can't afford to spend forty-eight hours at a stretch in the hope that I might get one run from a big carp.

But, back to the other night.

For a few days beforehand I took some soaked butter beans up to the water and scattered them around one or two swims. I had two reasons for doing this: first, I had always felt that butter beans would be a good carp bait but had never tried them. Secondly, I felt that there was a need for a change of bait on this water. The carp had been fairly hammered with potatoes and floating crust and were getting wise, while the small rudd and roach have always made short work of any paste or bread baits fished on the bottom.

I wanted a bait that was different and fairly immune from the attentions of small fish. Big but not too big. Tough enough to deter the tiddlers but not too tough for a carp to manage. Butter beans fitted the bill and were in fact one of the very few baits I could think of in the nature of a change. I won't say I had any great confidence in them but I was encouraged by the bubbles that appeared in the areas where I'd introduced them. The water was coloured and well stirred-up and the rushes nearby looked as if they'd been well investigated.

I don't know if other people do this, but I invariably bait down *in* the rush-beds as well as on the edge of them and into the open water. I think that carp spend a lot of their time in the rushes and that this way they are likely to find the bait quickly and be encouraged out into the open water in search of more.

It was quite dark when I put the rod in the rest and started to attach the luminous bobbin indicator. I doubt if the bait had been in position more than half a minute when the rod leapt towards the water. I know the bale arm *should* have been open but it wasn't. I was winding in slack line at the time so it couldn't have been. But only by the sheerest piece of good fortune did I have one of those rubber buttons on my bottom joint (I don't use them as a rule but this was an old rod) and it was that which I managed to grab hold of before the whole outfit went into the lake.

I'd heard of this happening with carp, but I never saw a rod do such a beautiful take-off before. And that was only a five-pounder!

It did some knitting with two other lines before I got it out (the friend I was with was using two rods) and it was half an hour before we sorted it all out. Then things really livened up.

Those beans were really on the menu that night. We had eleven bites which actually resulted in connections, and several more which we missed. I cannot remember a night's carp fishing that produced anything like as many bites. But here's the sad part. For some strange reason only one more fish, an eight-pounder, was landed. The rest came adrift after a few minutes on the hook.

Now it is a strange fact that of all the carp-fishing nights I can remember, those which have produced the most bites have invariably produced the most losses and this night was no exception. Many of my carp-fishing friends have recorded similar happenings and they say that they either miss or lose fish on these exceptional nights.

Does anyone know why? I don't.

Of course the beans *did* blunt the hooks and it isn't too easy to sharpen a hook with a big bean already on it. So that may have helped.

There are lots of things I could have done, of course. Like using soft beans for hookbait; like having something to put a hole through them before putting them on the hook; like using some particularly wide-gape hooks to keep the points clear—and so on. But of course you only think of these things afterwards, when you've encountered problems you didn't know existed before.

I hope I shall be able to try out some of those ideas but I doubt if there'll be another night like that for a long time to come.

Still, it's given me something to think about.

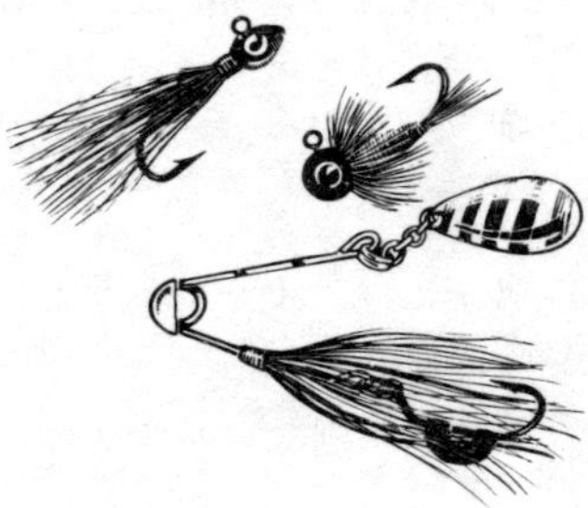

A Touch of Nostalgia

The kids that live across the road have a fair assortment of tackle between them and a number of fishable waters near to hand. They also have enough ready cash at times to enable them to take the bus and fish waters like Tring occasionally. They have good bikes and plenty of energy and, though they *never* seem to have any hooks (they're always scrounging them off me), they ought to be well pleased with their lot. But they're not.

They're always wanting to go somewhere different, and when they see me returning from a trip to Norfolk or Hampshire they're obviously envious and let me know in no uncertain terms what a lucky bloke I am to be able to go to places where the fish are bigger and easy to catch!

I *know* I'm lucky to have my sophisticated equipment and tackle, and my opportunities to fish a hundred distant waters if I so choose, but it wasn't always like that, and I keep trying to tell them so.

When I was a kid I had a beat-up old rod, a beat-up old bike and a few odds and ends of tackle. My fishing was confined to the local brook because that was the only free water available to me. I could only fish ticket and club waters when I had the money to buy permits, which wasn't often. As a consequence I really learned to understand that little brook and I seldom failed to catch fish because I was so familiar with it.

There has been much water under that low road-bridge since those days and my fishing has changed a great deal, but I wonder if I'd have fared any better had I been able to fish other waters and used better tackle in my early days?

Sometimes, the great choice of waters I have today actually puts me at a disadvantage because I find myself wondering all the time if I should be somewhere else. The truth is I have too much opportunity compared with those early days. Then I had no reason to wonder. If I wanted to fish I had but one choice. It was the brook or nothing, and I reckon, on reflection, that it was a good thing.

I have great difficulty in trying to convince the kids that this is so, however, and I'm sure they don't believe me when I tell them they'll do better to stay with one water, instead of trying so hard to flit from one to the other as they do. The grass is always greener . . . I suppose it always will be.

No one can blame the kids for wanting better things but, when such a wide choice of fishing is available, the issues become blurred and the business of making decisions as where to go and what to fish for becomes increasingly difficult. It's a whole lot easier then to end up with a blank because the distant water appears, at the time, to be the more inviting. Blanks are part of any angler's life, and I accept them with a certain philosophy, but blanks that come after a long drive in the early hours of the morning and a return journey after dark are much less acceptable! It's then that I sometimes wish I had but two nearby waters to fish—a pond and a stream.

I know very well that when I was in this position I understood my waters better and I could usually avoid being water-licked. And I keep trying to impress on young anglers that they'll learn more in the long run by coming to terms with waters they know and can reach easily. Let me quote a recent example.

Early one year I planned to fish locally for pike but, after a great deal of preparation, decided instead to make a long trip to Hampshire. The early-morning frost put me off as much as anything else because I figured (and my experience of the water should have told me differently) that the pike would be 'off'. In fact, the pike were 'on' as I learned later, while the roach of the distant Hampshire chalkstream were decidedly 'off'.

That, of course, is the luck of the game and it could have been the other way about, but had I *not* had the choice I'd have saved a lot of petrol and probably caught a lot of pike.

These thoughts were going through my mind recently when I fished a tiny stream, an off-shoot of the River Thame. It's a water I've known since childhood and it's seen more abstraction and pollution than most over the years, but it still beckons me occasionally. Where I once used to swim and catch big roach I can now cross in gumboots (except in times of flood), and the long glides where I used to trot a float at three feet are now little more than narrow ditches, but there are still some wide corners left and in times of high water fish accumulate there.

There's no road or track to the stretch I wanted to fish, and I figured that, after the holidays, the long walk across four meadows would do me no harm. I needed the exercise, but I decided to travel light (one rod and a minimum of tackle as in the old days) and I was truly looking forward to the hike more than the fishing. It just wasn't to be, however.

'Dump your gear in the Land-Rover,' said the farmer. 'I'll run you down.' And while I appreciated the offer and found it impossible to refuse, it just wasn't the way I wanted it. I wanted to walk that route with about the same amount of gear as I'd done in my early fishing days and try to re-live some old memories. (There'd have been no offer of a lift in those days—a chasing would have been more likely!)

The truth, of course, (although I didn't realise it when I was young) was that getting there was part of the fun; and the fact that it was a long and difficult journey made me appreciate the fishing more than ever.

I sat on the wide bend by the big willow tree and fished a one-shot float in the slow current under the far bank. Little roach came popping out like corks from a bottle and while they were only livebait size it was good fun on ultra-light tackle.

It took about an hour to empty the hole and I moved on to the next bend where the obvious hotspot was right at my feet. Again I popped out little roach like they were going out of style and then, when bites stopped altogether, I let the tackle hang in the stream half a rod's length out. Three bites produced three immature perch and I put them back with loving care.

What a great pleasure it was to see those little 'stripeys', and although as a kid I'd probably have cursed them I was glad to see them back. They *are* coming back here and there, I'm pleased to say, and there may come a time when I'll curse them again, but without little perch there can be no big ones—and I miss my big perch.

And, of course, I cannot help thinking of their great value as far as young anglers are concerned. Thousands of youngsters learned the rudiments of fishing, served their early apprenticeship years, and developed into good anglers because little perch were *always* there to be caught, And I cannot think of a better setting for a budding young angler than a pond full of little perch. No great skill is involved and if left alone for long enough they'll usually hook themselves and end up on the bank. That's important to a youngster and I feel sure that a lot of them have found the other species too difficult in recent years and, as a result, have lost interest completely. Small perch have always played a big part in the general angling scene and I sincerely hope they're on the way back again.

Thinking there might possibly be a bigger perch hanging around, I pulled a couple of red worms out from under a cow pat and let one of them hang in the current for a spell, not really caring one way or the other but just relaxing in a brief spell of January sunshine.

The float dived under, the line tightened and the rod tip bent all at precisely the same moment (or so it seemed), and I hung on to a veritable monster. A chub of fourteen ounces. I've never seen a chub there before and while its size meant nothing to me, catching it took me back again to the days when it would have set me all a-tremble.

I wondered, as I walked back across the four meadows, negotiating stiles and deep-ploughed furrows on the way, whether the private lake, the sophisticated boat and sonar equipment, the expensive rods and all the trappings that go with them, could have given me any more pleasure than those few fish I caught from the little brook with the barest of essentials.

I don't think they could, but I know I'm going to find it hard to convince the local youngsters that I actually *enjoyed* catching small fish from a nearby water. They expect greater things of me than that—*their* standards are sometimes a bit difficult to live up to!

Accidental Perch

I often wonder these days if we get as much pleasure out of catching a fish by accident as we do if we settle down to catch, say, a barbel by design and succeed in doing so? Generally speaking our attitude tends to be one of specialisation, and I can recall times when I have been disappointed over an otherwise excellent specimen because I was fishing for something else at the time.

The numbers of biggish perch I've taken on spoons meant for pike are considerable but I've experienced very little pleasure in their capture in the past. The main reason I suppose is because even a three-pound perch stands very little chance of fighting its weight when it's on the end of a 10-pound line and has a three-inch spoon in its mouth.

I've caught a lot of fair perch by design rather than accident, and by fair I mean fish between two and nearly three pounds. They've come as the result of knowing a water and the conditions which normally produce good specimens. They've come because I've worked for them and planned my fishing to suit the conditions for the time of year, and so forth. I've been very pleased to catch a dozen perch in a day and to weigh at least four of them in at over two pounds apiece, but I've never managed to get anything really big in the perch line except by accident. The few three-pound-plus fish and the solitary perch over four pounds that I've caught in all my years as a fisherman have been sheer flukes—accidents that have happened while I've been fishing for something else. Perch are like that!

If we made any sort of a study of big perch catches over a number of years, we'd find, I'm sure, that the great majority of them were caught by accident. There are exceptions, of course. The big perch bonanza of Arlesey Lake in the early 1950s is a notable one and there have been others, but there are very few perch specialists as such and if the truth be told there are very few waters that produce big perch in any real numbers. It's really difficult to come to terms with super perch.

I think a two-pound perch is a *big* fish and I've always been delighted to catch one as long as it's been by design and not by accident. I can remember being able to set out to catch two-pounders with more than an even chance of success but I could never set out confidently to catch three-pounders. Four-pounders, to me, are as rare as icebergs in Hell and I believe that luck has played a big part in the capture of all but a very few of the specimens recorded over this weight.

Logically, then, I ought to be disappointed if I caught a big perch by accident these days, but of course things have changed over the past few years. In many places the perch has become a rare fish and at the moment I'm delighted to catch a perch of any size. I don't care very much whether I catch it by accident or design. That's why I was very pleased indeed to catch five perch one day when I was fishing for roach and rudd.

These perch were decidedly not specimens—the best of them weighed only about three ounces—but, in view of the fact that they turned up in a water where they had been absent for several years, they gave me almost as much pleasure as a three-pounder.

And it all made me think. We had seen no perch for several years and so we hadn't really fished for them. Perhaps there were some better fish around if we gave them a chance to show themselves? To try and find out a bit more I spent most of the next morning spinning across and around the pit in question. I had two three-quarter-pounders for my trouble and I am convinced that perch fishing is going to be on again in a year or two's time.

That just serves as one example of an accidental catch giving me, at least, a degree of pleasure. No more will I look with disgust on the two-pounder that latches on to my big pike plug (if ever it happens again) and say what a pity it is that I wasn't *trying* to catch it! From now on I shall be delighted to see each and every perch that comes along, irrespective of size. We've been short of perch for too long and I've missed 'em!

Accidental catches don't always disappoint, nor do they always delight their captors. I suppose it's all a matter of attitude. I can remember times when I've honestly and sincerely been bitterly disappointed over a number of five-pound-plus tench! It wasn't an act. It wasn't done to impress because there were no other anglers around to impress except Ken and Joe Taylor—my brother and our cousin—and I know they felt exactly the same as I did. Our one ambition at that time was to catch a carp—any carp at all—from Wotton Lakes. We worked desperately hard towards that end and we did everything we possibly could to avoid catching tench. The fact that we caught bigger and better tench through trying *not* to catch them was small consolation at the time.

We know now, of course, that our chances of catching carp were very slender and that we in fact wasted several seasons flogging away for carp that were virtually non-existent. We were disappointed at the time, but in spite of it all we learned a lot more about tench fishing, which has stood us in good stead ever since.

I smile now when I think of the great show we used to put on when one of us caught a bream in the middle of the night when we were carp fishing at another water. Some of those bream were good fish and we'd have been secretly pleased to catch them during the day. But to have a streaking run on a huge piece of paste in the middle of the night and to end up with a dreadful, smelly, slimy bream instead of a beautiful(?) big carp . . . !

I'm still not sure whether we really meant it or not, but I guess we had to appear disgusted to convince the others.

Nowadays, I try to enjoy all forms of fishing. (The only kind I can't enjoy is cod fishing from a boat. That is sheer hell as far as I'm concerned, but it's a disappointment to me not to be able to participate) and I find I have less and less time for specialisation. That's why I often find myself fishing in winter for anything that comes along. If a big old chub hangs on while I'm dace fishing that's fine. And if a barbel takes hold of my roach bait I'm not going to grumble or show disappointment. But I must confess that a fish I caught by sheer accident not long ago really did disappoint me. It was an eight-pound trout, the biggest I've ever caught in my life—but it was, of course, out of season! I caught it on two maggots, 2-pound line and a No. 14 hook. I didn't see it for at least fifteen minutes and the actual landing of it gave me immense pleasure. But what do I truthfully say now when someone asks me what's the biggest trout I've ever caught?

'Goer' Gudgeon

When I received an invitation to fish the River Loddon at a spot where I had last fished over twenty years previously, I had vivid memories of the roach, dace and gudgeon there, and wondered if I should see the water as I last saw it, or if I was to be disillusioned yet again.

I had fished there only once and, since that day, had never seen it again. I remembered how I had been impressed by the general size of the roach and dace, and more so by the fact that it looked like being a river I could quickly come to terms with. Being a small water, it had a special appeal. I had found it a delightful spot, and for many years I had had a yen to go back there. Sheer coincidence brought about the invitation from Alan Brown, my neighbour, and it wasn't until he began describing the water that I realised he was inviting me back to the same little river. There is a story attached to it, and I think that story is worth telling again.

At the time I worked for a Government department in Buckinghamshire, and out of the blue one winter came a challenge from a Government department in Hampshire. Bring a team of ten, they said, and fish against us on our own water. The details are vague after all this time, and if club records should prove me wrong regarding figures, the story itself is true enough.

I couldn't raise a team of ten from the establishment so I recruited two from outside—my cousin Joe and Dick Walker.

When we arrived at the water (referred to as the Loddon, but strictly speaking only a tributary), there was an immediate problem. We had a full team, but the challengers were two short.

Big-hearted as ever, I said that in view of the fact that it was only a friendly match, they could have one of our men to make up two equal sides.

'Good,' said the captain. 'We'll have Dick Walker—he used to work for us anyway!'

I will not go into the details of the match except to say that it was a size-limit affair, and that all day I kept returning monstrous gudgeon and keeping only sizeable roach and dace. I did fairly well, and, in fact, I believe my team won. But I was beaten to top weight by a few ounces by Dick. The real blow, however, was that part of his catch included gudgeon similar to those I'd been putting back.

'They all go,' said the steward. 'Five inches and over is sizeable.'

Served me right, I suppose, for not checking, but I swear I returned something like eighty gudgeon that day, many of which would have weighed in for me and given me top weight.

It didn't matter a scrap, of course. It was a great day with a nice gang of fellows, and my sneaky little trick of bringing in some outside talent was quickly rumbled.

I wondered, when I talked to Alan about going back there, if the gudgeon were still around.

'Yes,' he said, 'they are. Horrendous brutes, but the minnows are more of a problem.'

On both counts he was right. But what a great pleasure it was to me to go back and look at a lovely little river that had not changed much at all in all those years. I could even recognise the swim I'd fished all those years ago.

And I caught some of the gudgeon, minnows and dace as well.

I could not, in the short time available to me, get hold of the roach, but Alan, who knew the water a little better, had them going before I left at one o'clock. They were a good average size and one certainly topped the pound.

Maggots, Alan had said, only encouraged the minnows, and it was better to use casters. Hemp and casters for loose feed and two light-coloured casters for hookbait.

I couldn't recall ever having used the two baits mixed before but, of course, I took note.

There was hardly enough current to use my favourite old centre-pin—which is what I'd have liked—so I used a 2-pound line to a 1½-pound hook-link on a fixed-spool outfit.

The little wire-stemmed Avon float held true down the centre run and first trot down I was into a dace. No problems. This would be good.

But it went a bit sour after that. Notwithstanding Alan's doctrine, we both learned very quickly that minnows like casters as well as maggots. In fact there was no way of avoiding them that we knew.

The odd dace and gudgeon came our way but, for the most part, the minnows drove us crazy.

I told Alan how we used to beat them on the Ouse years ago. Stewed wheat was the bait. The roach and dace could handle it; the minnows gave it best. But, of course, we had no wheat.

Legered worm produced a lot of pecks and a few big gudgeon for me an hour or so later, but, when everything went strangely dead, we took the opportunity of walking the stretch and looking at some of the other swims. There was a dozen I wanted to try, and I reckoned that under some of the overhangs a legered crust cube would be deadly chub medicine in cold weather.

Returning to our rods, we found we had had visitors. A herd of inquisitive cattle had kicked over the tackle bags, upset the maggots, put slime on the thermos, and crunched a new fourteen-foot match rod lying there in its bag. I suppose it was our own fault, but those beasts were nowhere near when we left and nowhere near when we returned. They had come and gone like thieves in the night.

Rods can be repaired, however, and if it is really necessary you can always buy a new one, but nothing much can be done once a river has been ruined. The important aspect for me was that this little river had *not* changed. It was just as charming as ever and for that reason alone a broken rod was of little consequence.

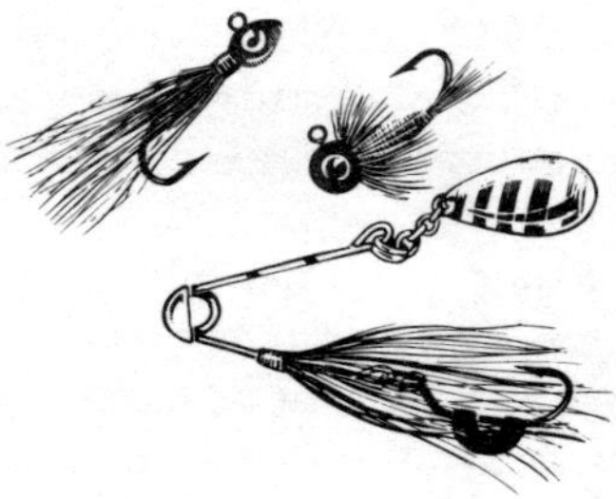

Eel Rites

My memory for places and people does not improve, but it is never entirely lost and I recall one old countryman telling a couple of friends and myself that an eel we'd just caught 'won't die till sunset, you know'. To which either Dick Walker or our friend Pete Thomas replied, 'Wanna bet?'; and fetched it an almighty clout across the back, just above the vent. The eel, I promise you, never moved again.

Another strange superstition about eels, which apparently cropped up in a television programme, is that an eel should be killed by being buried in a grave dug in the shape of a crucifix. Well, I have tried to kill eels by all means (except digging graves for them) and I've always found it to be a case of some you win, some you lose.

I 'killed' a netful of eels once up in Lancashire when I was awaiting demobilisation. To keep the peace with my comrades I hung the net outside the barrack room window and in the morning the camp cook had them all swimming in his deep sink before he dressed them out. After the treatment I'd dished out to those eels I can only marvel at their powers of survival.

Other eels caught more recently failed to live the night through in a roomy keepnet held in a cold chalkstream. There's no way I can feel sure about anything to do with eels except that I have never tasted a bad one.

My paternal grandmother and all those around her were passionately fond of eels, but their preparation involved an unchanging ritual. First, the eel was not allowed to die. It had to be kept alive until it could be dealt with correctly. I can still hear my old aunt Sis (I never knew her real name) saying, 'Ain't that a lovely eel, my cock; put it in the sink!' So, too, I dare bet, can Dick Walker.

'That one,' we would say when we caught an extra big one, 'will do for Aunt Sis.'

The eel, poor wretch, had to be placed in a bath with a block of crushed rock salt. Then its tail was cut in two places, about two inches apart. The salt, I remember, turned crimson and the eel died. Then it was nailed through the head to the fence, the skin around the throat was cut lightly through the flesh, peeled back and pulled off with a piece of rough towelling. The skin was then somehow dried out and made into wrist straps which were supposed to help ease rheumatic pains. But that, and the superstition of the grave, adds even more to the mystery and mumbo-jumbo that surrounds the common eel.

I did not see the TV programme in which an eel was interred in a cruciform grave, and while I do not doubt the sincerity of those who believe such things, I can only regard the idea as utterly crazy. Even if it works (and I'm not saying it doesn't) who, in their right mind, would go to the trouble of digging graves to kill eels? ('Sorry, I can't come to tea, Vicar; I've just caught this eel and I've got to dig a grave for it!')

Perhaps I'm heartless, perhaps I believe an eel that has been skinned, gutted and chopped up, is hardly likely to feel much, even if it *is* still wriggling in the pan! Perhaps I believe that the old London commercial eel establishments know a thing or two. They want their eels *alive*.

There are anglers, and I know one or two personally, who believe that if an eel dies through lack of oxygen, or if it does not survive the journey home, it is no longer fit to eat. I am the first to agree that I like my fish fresh, and this means all my fish, but I do not think I would worry too much if I found one had died in the wet sack on the way home. After all, a great many sea-caught fish are left to die. Pollack, cod, bass, to name a few, end up in the bottom of the boat when the fishing is 'hot'.

No one has time either to kill them or to keep them alive: it's a case of get them while the going's good. Later, on the way back in they are cleaned and gutted. They may have been dead for a few hours, but they *are* still very freshly caught fish.

One point that probably hasn't been mentioned is that, despite their tenacity, eels can apparently die from sheer exhaustion. I have had several experiences which help bear this out, and I am puzzled by it all.

If an eel in a fast chalkstream is hooked and becomes weeded to such an extent that a long time is needed to get it to the bank, there is more than an even chance that it will be completely dead on arrival. It has happened to me several times, whereas those eels landed quickly from the same water during the same night have still been full of fight next morning. Is it possible, I wonder, to drown an eel?

I once had a half-hour-long tussle with a small conger eel (of six to eight pounds) which I hooked off the rocks in the early hours of the morning on the Fowey River. There was no frantic screaming of reels or such, but a simple and monotonous see-saw pulling back and forth, with me gaining a foot of line then losing it seconds later. It was like pulling against strong elastic. Eventually, the light of a torch and the receding tide revealed that the eel was in a crack between the rocks. Its head would appear briefly when I put on the strain and then it would withdraw out of sight again the second I relaxed to try and gain more line.

When the tide dropped below where the eel had taken refuge, the fight still went on and only ended when my companion decided to join in. He waited some twelve feet above the eel with a rock poised in both hands and on his intructions I heaved the head clear. He dropped the rock on it, and the whole eel popped out like a cork from a bottle. Normally a little tap on the head like that would have made no difference to such an eel. This one never moved again and I am convinced it died from sheer exhaustion. Well, one of us had to have some relief!

Eels are weird creatures and there is much about them that we still do not understand, which is why I would not ridicule anything said or written about them. I *know* they travel across land, I *know* they have a sense of direction which we find hard to understand. But there are many other weird and wonderful things that happen in nature.

My five-year-old granddaughter, for instance, can find water with a divining rod. She doesn't know what she's doing—she thinks it's just a super game—and if we're all truthful, none of us really knows. Perhaps it's as well we don't. Besides, those little mysteries that surround our eels make them all the more interesting to catch.

If you really want to kill an eel quickly, of course, you can chop off its head. Then you can have the very doubtful pleasure of trying to skin it afterwards. It's not really very difficult—it's just about impossible!

Turning to Trout

I took a couple of trout round to a friend some weeks ago and he was more pleased than if I'd given him a ten-pound note. 'These will go straight into the freezer for a special occasion,' he told me.

My friend is a coarse fisherman, and a good one, so I was a bit puzzled as to why he should get excited over a couple of two-pound trout. 'If you like 'em all that much,' I asked 'why don't you go out and catch some for yourself?'

His reply ought to have surprised me but it didn't because I'd heard it so many times before from other people. 'I'd never get the hang of it,' he said. 'All this business of learning to cast all over again and having to study the insect life so as to be able to copy it, and so forth, would take up too much of my time. And anyway it's all above my head.'

I won't tell you what I said to him, and in any event it isn't printable, but it meant in effect that my young friend was talking nonsense.

Let's get a few things straight about trout fishing, however, before someone decides that I'm being either big-headed or guilty of over-simplifying things. I was not suggesting to my friend that all this study of entomology and the like is kid's stuff and that anyone can pick it up in five minutes. Nor was I suggesting that he could learn to fly-cast with precision and accuracy within five minutes. I've been practising for years now and there's very little in the way of precision or accuracy in my fly-casting—but I still manage to catch quite a lot of trout. And it's my opinion that other coarse fishers, who, like me, have very limited skill and knowledge on the subject could do the same.

There's a lot written about the finer points of trout fly presentation, strict imitation and all the rest of it, which to the average down-to-earth coarse fisherman is so much Chinese, but which he tends to regard as essential and beyond his capabilities. It isn't essential these days. It may have been so years ago when nearly all trout fishing was practised on clear chalkstreams, and the fish were wild brown trout. Or so-called wild brown trout. The truth is that a great many of those were introduced from stock ponds too, but for some reason they were still regarded as resident fish.

I'm the first to admit that if you're confined to dry fly and nymph only, the brown trout of clear rivers can be very difficult to catch and it may be necessary then for you to cast very accurately and be able to imitate the natural fly on the water. Brown trout, especially big brown trout, can be extremely difficult to catch if you're restricted regarding method. They wouldn't be so hard if you were allowed to do your own thing occasionally! Why do you think these restrictions were imposed in the first place? This sort of fishing is out on its own. It's practised by people who enjoy deceiving trout into believing that the fly they've presented is the real thing. It requires skill and, more important, it's the way those people *enjoy* fishing; but it isn't necessary to go to all that trouble to catch enough trout for the table and have a great deal of fun doing so.

The rainbow trout in stillwater and river fisheries all over the country are far easier to catch, and although some folk will try to tell you how essential it is to study what they're eating, and so forth, with a view to presenting an imitation nymph, shrimp, snail or whatever, at the right depth and speed, on tackle fine enough to allow the offering to behave naturally in front of the fish, believe me it isn't. It's very commendable, and if you're clever enough it's a delightful way of catching rainbows, but don't let anyone kid you that it's ever essential to go to such lengths.

Rainbows are pretty predatory creatures and they're apparently hungry for ninety per cent of the time. The way to catch them is the same as it is with chub. You get to them without being seen and you put something across their bows that looks either like food, or a little fish that's going to join in and have some of the action itself. A rainbow will usually nail a minnow that looks like invading the food supply, and that's probably why a streamer fly is so deadly when the rainbows themselves are nymphing or rising to surface flies. Even when you see them rising to mayflies or any other particularly thick hatch of surface flies, you need not feel at a disadvantage because you have no strict imitations in your fly box.

I once caught a limit of free-rising rainbows during a big hatch of surface fly by stripping back a big black-and-white lure deep. I didn't do it because I couldn't offer a surface fly, but rather to prove for myself that it wasn't necessary to do so. Brown trout may ignore such offerings in similar circumstances, but rainbows are different. They often remain hidden, and seemingly not very much interested in food, but they come to life like all other fish once a steady stream of food comes their way. They differ from other fish, however, in that they do not necessarily become preoccupied with that particular food source. Once they've *started* feeding they're liable to take anything, and if a streamer or bucktail fly gets near enough to them to cause irritation, they'll have it.

I know, of course, that freshly introduced stock-fish are a lot easier to catch than fish that have been in some time, but what I have said still applies. I have caught rainbows which I know to have wintered twice (and which, by then, were virtually wild fish) by applying this kind of approach.

I've caught them on popping bug flies (an American cork- or wooden-bodied fly that causes a surface disturbance when twitched) while they've been rising to some kind of black gnat or hawthorn fly. I've caught them on black lures when they've been nymphing gracefully just below the surface. And I've worried them into coming out of a weed-bed shelter when they've not been feeding at all. They are very much like salmon in that they will come back to their lie and rest even after disturbance; and if you don't succeed at the first attempt you can often keep at it till you do.

I do not suggest that all rainbows on all waters can be treated this way. All I know is that those in all the waters I fish do. So I do not pay too much attention to those who tell me that I should spoon out the stomach contents of my fish to find out what they're feeding on. And I tend to pay more attention to finding the fish without them first finding me.

What *does* spooning out a fish really achieve? It proves only one thing to me: it proves that the fish I have in my hand, dead, was feeding on, say, black midge pupae, and that I *ought* possibly to have caught it on a buzzer tied on a No. 16. Trouble is, I caught it on a muddler minnow! So if, in the first instance, strict imitation was not necessary to catch the fish, why should it be necessary to catch others? And who's to say that, because this one fish was feeding on black midge pupae, all the others are too?

The truth, of course, is that there are always at least three or four food sources for the trout of any water, and certain groups of fish settle down to exploit certain sources as and when they are present. Thus, there will always be some fish which prefer insects, some which prefer to grub around the bottom for larvae, snails, etc., and some which apparently prefer to chase fry.

I'm not suggesting that they *never* have a change or that they do what they've chosen to do all the time. That would defeat my own argument. What I *do* suggest, however, is that without a great deal of entomological knowledge you can tie almost any fly on the end of a line, cast it out and pull it back in the vicinity of a rainbow trout with a good chance of the fish hanging on to it.

That's what my young friend did—after I'd convinced him that he could. He spent ten minutes on the lawn with a fly rod and the following weekend went out and caught three rainbows for himself. He likes trout fishing now!

The Con Trick

Trout fishing in the early morning isn't everyone's idea of fun but I have a feeling that if you know exactly where a big trout lies you may catch it by fishing its lie stealthily and without a lot of rod swishing. If you don't know the exact lie of this big fish you cannot put your offering in the right place; to do the job properly you have to be very accurate and you don't get too many chances.

The little loaded shrimps I use are deadly, but they have to be put right in front of the trout otherwise they're not noticed. Then they have to be made to rise up in the water so that the sudden movement is spotted by the trout. I believe the experts call it the 'induced take', and I can see the reason why. The reaction of the trout seems not to stem from any real desire to feed upon whatever it is that moves in front of it, but rather it is 'conned' into taking it because of its natural tendency to snap at passing food. The same sort of thing happens when you drop a big, black, juicy slug just behind a lazy old chub. He doesn't really stop to think (unless he's been caught that way before) but turns and grabs while the opportunity is still there.

Now, it is obvious that if you can *see* a trout idling in the current you can do something about putting a nymph or a shrimp to it, but if you *can't* see it, you have to *know* exactly where it is hiding before you can hope to do any 'inducing'.

Apart from that rather special situation, however, I have the general impression that there's not a lot of advantage to be gained from trout fishing at crack of dawn except on reservoirs. The fish don't show very much as a rule and they're not easy to spot in the early-morning light. When the sun shows itself very early, the long shadows thrown on the water quickly scare the trout and send them back under weed cover. All in all, early-morning trout fishing in clear streams does not seem to be worthwhile, but I prefer to do my fishing early rather than late, because I have long since given up hopes of seeing an evening rise. I don't believe there are such things. People invent them just to fool the likes of me!

One particular morning, however, I shall remember for a long time. The fish were showing early, and at about nine o'clock they were rising along the whole of the stretch. There was no regularity about it, but there was activity the whole time.

I caught two big rainbows very quickly and then, just as quickly as it started, the action ceased and the stream went dead. I returned to see if I could again spot a big one I'd seen earlier but he was still asleep somewhere, and I made my way back to the car for breakfast.

A big brown trout appeared from below a patch of weed, saw me, and tucked itself away out of sight again. But I *knew* where it was, and marked it for later.

After breakfast I spotted another big brown as it showed briefly further downstream before settling under the near bank. I froze and let it rest a moment or two before casting to it. It was lying deep, but I could see it fairly clearly from my position downstream, and I noticed that it moved out from the bank occasionally to inspect or intercept something in the current. I cast to it and the shrimp entered the water close to the bank a couple of yards above where it was lying. At that precise moment the trout decided to move downstream and out of my sight. I don't think I frightened it, but I shall never know. There was a swirl and a flash of silver as another fish moved out from cover and hit my shrimp with enthusiasm that almost tore the rod from my hand!

There was a moment's confusion and then, twenty yards downstream of me, a big rainbow jumped clear of the water. A second or two later the backing showed on my reel as the fish carried on downstream and jumped yet again. I chased after it, and tried to pick up some line, amazed that we were still connected. Fortunately, the bank at this point was clear of trees and bushes and I was able to get below the fish eventually. Finally, having got it under some sort of control, I held it hard as it tried to head upstream against the strong current. This knocked the stuffing out of it and it was soon in the net.

I thought at first I might have caught my first seven-pounder, but when I weighed it, the scales recorded a quarter of a pound less. I strung the fish with the other two and went back to look for the big brown I'd seen earlier.

It was lying in a narrow channel, a foot below the surface in a thick bunch of weed. It was huge, and it was feeding!

My green nymph dropped in front of it and I lifted the rod point slowly as I drew in the slack. No need for a second try. No preliminaries, no hesitation. That trout wanted the nymph and he took it at once.

The situation again became confused as the fish moved off upstream, taking a great patch of weed with it. By another stroke of luck this came adrift when the action slowed down, otherwise I'm sure I'd have lost everything. As it was, another patch of weed fouled the line and slid down over the trout, almost covering it, and certainly preventing it from seeing. That stopped its flight altogether, and I netted both the fish and about half a hundredweight of weed at the same time.

It weighed 5 pounds 13 ounces and beat my previous best brown trout by over 1½ pounds.

It takes a lot to set me trembling these days (which is, of course, a great pity) but when I looked at those four trout and realised that two of them were personal bests, and when I considered that they weighed a total of 20 pounds 10 ounces and *averaged* 5 pounds 2 ounces, I admit that I was stricken by a touch of the shakes! Perhaps I had more than my fair share of luck, but I doubt if I'll ever have a day to better it.

Too Easy

We intended to fish for trout during the day and then stay on all night to fish the main river for eels. The keeper had given us permission and we'd got the whole deal laid on nicely. I'd collected a nice lot of small rudd baits and put them in deep freeze in advance. We'd caught five good trout and we were going to dress them out and use the innards as groundbait.

There's this deep hole just below the fishing hut and every salmon that gets caught is gutted and cleaned just above it. The offal all drifts down and comes to rest in the deep hole, and it's a real natural for eels. Whenever I go there and have a few minutes to spare, I chuck a piece of bait out and usually get an eel of some sort almost immediately. I've never had a big one, but most of them are big enough to eat and they're the best eels I've ever tasted. So I thought perhaps that a full night's session would be great fun and give us another chance to make good some of our previous promises. But everything went sour on us.

The heavens fairly opened at about seven o'clock in the evening and it then rained solidly for twelve hours. Not for a hundred eels would I have sat out fishing in that lot! There was no shelter and we hadn't brought our umbrellas so we sat in the car for a while and hoped for a let-up, which never came.

Having finally decided to postpone the eel fishing for the time being, we went to collect the trout. We'd put the trout on two clip-type stringers and left them in the river as is our usual practice. This keeps them nice and clean and doesn't allow them to dry out or get sticky and fly-blown. (I've seen so many trout chucked up the bank and left to deteriorated.) But today we slipped up. We'd left one stringer holding two fish on a long line in the steady current just above the weir, and when we went to retrieve them they were wedged tightly, deep down under the weir gate. There was obviously all sorts of weed and debris down there and the whole stringer was jammed solid. A big patch of floating weed must have fouled the stringer and dragged it downstream into the incredibly fast current that went through the gates and we were unable to shift it. Eventually the string broke and we had to say goodbye to two nice trout.

Things weren't going too well for us, but we cheered up when we decided to go and fish our own little trout water. I'm always being accused of having my own private waters and so forth, and in nine cases out of ten it simply isn't true. But this little trout stream really is private. I share it with a good friend, and we both agreed when we took it on that we'd keep it exclusively to ourselves and one guest each.

In order to explain just what this is all about I should perhaps go back to last spring when I first got to know of its existence. By a sheer stroke of luck I was having a quiet drink with this particular friend when it was mentioned in passing by the landlord of the pub. Introductions followed, and then we went to see the water. It was in a delightful setting, chalk-based and running through watercress beds before widening into a deep wide moat. There were no fish in it at all as far as the owner knew but it had been stocked years ago and neglected for the past two or three. Trout had reached four pounds in it to his certain knowledge, he told us.

Without a lot of preliminaries we settled on an annual rental and finally acquired the fishing rights on a water devoid of fish. Not that it mattered.

A telephone call in the right quarter quickly organised some fish, and after a few days we introduced a hundred and fifty mixed brown and rainbow trout. Vast quantities of weed had sprung up in the crystal-clear water by that time and it was obvious that there would be plenty of food available for the fish.

There and then I shut them from my mind. I had no intention of fishing for them for a long time—at least until they had lost their tameness. That was roughly two months ago and, rightly or wrongly, Ken and I decided that we were now entitled to go and cast a fly to them.

It had stopped raining by the following morning and we stood and 'studied form' for a while as a weak sun tried to break through. There was a plop upstream as a fish rose. Another downstream. Another and another under the willows on the far bank and we put up our little brook rods hastily lest the rise should stop. Ten minutes later we took them down again sadly and decided that we hadn't the heart for such carryings on! I don't know how many fish we caught and released but I guess it must have been a dozen or so. Every fly that hit the water was seized immediately and, although those trout had grown enormously in so short a time and were full of spirit, they still behaved like tame fish. I suppose that's just what they are, really.

I've never believed in catching and returning trout. I think that good fishing can deteriorate if fish are continually caught and released, and I agree one hundred per cent with those fishery owners who insist that all fish caught should be removed.

I wonder, however, if, here, we haven't got a situation which demands a re-think. These fish are so easy to catch that we could strip the water in no time at all if we fished it for an hour at a time and killed all we caught. Would it not be better in this instance, I ask myself, to give them a bit of a dusting and teach them a few lessons? I really don't like the idea, but nor do I like the thought of catching suicidal trout!

The real answer I suppose is to write them off completely this year and hope that they'll winter well and put on weight for next season. Of those we caught the other day, Ken and I killed two. They were stuffed full of food in the form of snails and shrimps. Their flesh was pink and they were in super condition. They weighed just about a pound each; with luck they'll be double that weight next season. My experience of trout stocking and trout fishery management is precisely nil, but I do enjoy trout fishing as long as it provides me with some sort of challenge.

Looking back over that weekend I have to admit it wasn't very exciting, but I've never before been disappointed because the fish were too easy! And, by the way, going back to those two trout on the stringer, Ken overheard two trout fishers talking three days later. He was then over a hundred miles from where it had all happened, but what he heard one say was: 'I found this chain thing with two trout clipped to it, washed up under the bank. Can't think who'd have done such a thing!'

Well, at least we know the end of the story—which is something, I suppose.

Fun in a Flood

I've never been over excited about flood-water fishing, but there are few occasions when I regard the situation as absolutely hopeless. I've always felt that the fish had to stay in the river somewhere and that if they could be found they could probably be caught. There are exceptions, of course. Cold flood water consisting mainly of melted snow *never* impressed me, and I soon learned to stay at home when those conditions prevailed. I can recall odd fish taken from time to time, of course, but generally speaking I reckon that if the living-room needs painting then's the time to do it!

The other week, the trout stream was in flood—higher and more coloured than I've ever seen it before, and when my brother Ken and I arrived at daybreak I didn't rate our chances at all. It's a different situation, of course. In a thick flood water there are lots of dodges you can try for coarse fish. Traditional lobtails or strong cheese paste will sooner or later produce a few pecks if you put them in the right spot. And, generally speaking, the right spots are indicated by the level and flow of the water. Coarse fish hole up in comfortable spots. Sometimes those comfortable spots are dead slacks, but more often they're little refuge areas out of the main current. I always try to find a spot where the current is about the same speed as it is in a productive swim in normal conditions and I often end up fishing a spot that's rarely if ever fished during the rest of the year.

It doesn't always work, of course, but at least it forms the basis of a start; and if the fish aren't there to begin with, there's a chance that the right baits and groundbaits will draw them in later. But there's no way you can play that game on a trout stream when you're restricted to fly fishing.

Both Ken and I know the usual trout lies and over the years we've learned how to exploit them fairly well. Most times we can see our fish, and by practising a little stealth we are usually able to winkle one or two of them out, but today we could see nothing. Even the streamer weed-beds were lost in the dirty water and it soon became apparent that the trout had either moved out of their lies or were tucked away and strictly 'off'.

We couldn't apply any real water lore, but at least we figured out some of the places where the fish were hiding. It was, in fact, a typical coarse-fishing situation. They were not in the slacks as such, but they *were* in the slower-moving water, resting up out of the main current in spots they do not normally inhabit. This really meant that very little real casting was necessary and short flicks upstream close to the bank were all that were necessary. But it was a blind kind of fishing. The excitement of stalking a big trout, covering it carefully, keeping out of sight and manipulating the cast so that the nymph, shrimp or whatever, would almost bounce on its nose, were all missing. We were fishing hopefully but with no certain knowledge that trout were within casting distance.

In a deep, slow, run almost under my very feet I hooked a biggish fish that belted off downstream at a rate of knots and then, for no apparent reason, stopped and moved around rather aimlessly under pressure. It was a strong fish, fighting every inch of the way, but it never really tried to go anywhere. The long, long runs up or downstream we've learned to expect from these trout didn't materialise, and I thought perhaps it was because the fish couldn't actually *see* where it was going.

It is possible, I suppose, but as it had somehow managed to spot my little wet fly and nail it, I wouldn't like to be too dogmatic. That fish weighed $4\frac{1}{4}$ pounds. Another from the same spot shortly afterwards weighed four pounds exactly, and behaved similarly. I was gloating a bit because I'd got a couple of fish and Ken had so far failed to connect. But, as usual, I was counting my chickens!

'There's a *big* fish here,' said Ken. 'It swirled at my fly and sheered off again. It's tucked away under the tree roots, I think, and there's no way I can reach it from here. You'll have to try it from there.'

He was excited. Almost hopping around on one foot in fact.

'Come on over here,' he called. 'I know just where it is, and you'll get it from where you are. I can't get anywhere near it . . . I've hooked it!'

All without stopping for breath.

It *was* a big fish, and unlike my two it made off downstream at a frightening rate, heading for the little waterfall where the current was really hurtling down. Had it reached there and gone over the top all would have been lost, but by sheer luck I happened to be there before it arrived. I plunged the net into the water directly in its path, thinking perhaps it might swim straight into it; but it knew all about nets.

My action did, however, have the desired effect of turning it away from the danger spot. It changed direction and made a very long run upstream into the fast water above. Then it tore downstream again and yet again. In all, I deterred it from going over the top eight times! I had it in the net (well, most of it) three different times but still it managed to escape, and every time I looked at it, it seemed to grow.

The little fly was fully visible in the side of its mouth and seemed to be holding by a piece of skin. I noticed the fly was yellow and I also noticed Ken's face was green!

At last my real chance came and I got the net immediately below it, lifted, shook, made the fish fold up almost double and heaved it ashore. At that point the hook came out, and Ken developed a severe case of the shakes. Someone had hooked that fish before. A small fly and an inch of fine leader were still in its mouth when we inspected it further.

Ken removed it and stuck it in his hat for a keepsake. We weighed the fish back at the car; it scaled exactly eight pounds, and was a personal best for Ken which pleased us both.

After that, of course, the rain and the wind and the cold and the floods didn't matter any more. We'd *both* had a lot of fun with that one fish.

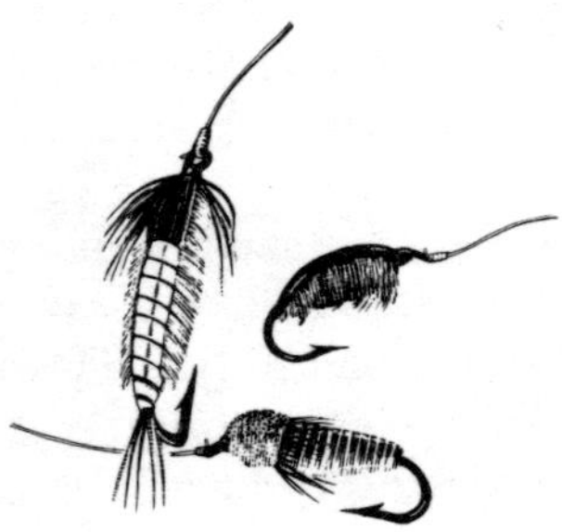

Team-Work

Ken and Malcolm Baldwin joined me trout fishing on the little stream a couple of weeks ago. We set off at four o'clock in the morning so as to have covered the hundred miles by six, and thus avoid the happy holiday traffic. There's no real advantage in getting to a trout water of this nature very early except perhaps to try for a really good fish you've had your eye on for some time. Such big fish are hard to approach during the daytime and they seldom join in in any general rise during the evening, but if you know more or less exactly where one lies you can often sneak up on it in the early hours and catch it before it 'wakes up'.

Ken had such a fish spotted and was anxious to have first crack at it. We left him to it and, true to form, he came back shortly with a six-pound rainbow that he had taken on a little loaded shrimp. I caught a mere pounder in the meantime, with Malcolm spotting for me on the opposite bank.

Malcolm was new to fly fishing and had done very well in the short time he'd been doing it, but he told me that it was much more fun spotting and watching the fish for someone else. I knew what he meant because it's something Ken and I do quite a lot. There are many situations, on the small stream, where one man can see a fish and be in a position to direct the other on such matters as, for instance, the line of cast.

He can see the fish, he can see the fly or nymph or shrimp, and can tell the other exactly how to place it next cast so that it's directly in the trout's vision. Furthermore, he can watch the reaction of the fish, tell whether or not it has shown interest, and on more than one occasion Ken has been able to tell me when to strike, knowing that the trout has taken before I've realised it myself.

It may well be that the registration would have reached me at the rod end a brief second afterwards, but sometimes the registration on the line comes too late. The trout has rejected the fly by then and the strike doesn't connect.

I'm very much aware of my failings in this field. It takes an expert nymph fisherman to *anticipate* the take of a trout in deepest water when he can't actually see it. There are many who can, but while I would, perhaps, hook one out of three takes, I do not profess to be that efficient.

But there's more to it than that. It's a way of enjoying one's fishing even more, and, of course, each fish caught is a pleasure shared. Ken and I, when we go together, often assemble only one rod despite the fact that we're both entitled to fish in our own right. The stream is narrow and by means of a careful approach we select fish and catch them by team work.

If I have the rod and I can see a fish that's easier for Ken to reach, I toss the rod over to him and tell him where to cast. We both carry landing nets and there have been many occasions when I've hooked a fish on one bank and steered it to Ken's landing net on the opposite one. And, of course, vice-versa. I caught a five-pounder that way earlier this season.

There's nothing new about the idea, of course. On the small rivers we fish for dace, roach and occasionally chub, it's often possible to apply the same tactics with maggots or stewed wheat.

Most of the time the fish lie up in clear water and are slow to start feeding. Sending down a shotted float after the first scattering of loose maggots tends to put them off rather than encourage them, and it pays, if you can arrange it, to have a friend watching from a hidden vantage point and giving a running commentary on their reactions.

It's of very little use being too anxious to start fishing. The thing to do is to get the fish feeding first and on clear rivers this often takes a long time.

You can, if you're energetic enough, and you've enough cover to conceal your movements, move from the upstream spot to where the fish are located and watch the proceedings for yourself. But it's easier if you have someone else to do the watching brief for you.

The rate of introduction of loose maggots is very critical and it's easy to overdo it. If you put in too many you'll find the fish drop back after those they've missed, and it's so much easier if you have someone opposite the swim to tell you where the maggots are going. If you're too sparing, however, the fish may move up towards the source of introduction and eventually become suspicious.

Get things just right, however, and you can have the fish eagerly exploiting every loose maggot that comes through and once they're really working you can begin to fish.

And here's where your spotter again comes in very useful. He can tell you how the fish are reacting to the hookbait. I've spotted many times myself and I've sometimes noticed that every loose maggot has been taken while the hookbait has been ignored. The presentation has obviously been wrong. The float is too conspicuous, perhaps, or the tackle is not fine enough to allow the bait to behave naturally in the current, the shotting needs adjusting, maybe, or some other minor detail needs attending to before the action can really start. And don't ever think that spotting is not as much fun as actually catching the fish. It is. And very often it's a lot more exciting.

Remember that as a spotter you can see the fish and that you're the one who's actually getting them on the hook. You're the one who's experiencing the frustrations, the near-misses and the real excitement of seeing the fish take the bait a brief second before it registers at the float. The angler upstream is simply obeying instructions—he's *your* tool, employed in the business of catching *your* fish. And even a 'goer'-sized dace becomes an achievement in these circumstances. Everything is magnified when you can direct the tackle to select a monster from a shoal of smaller fish.

You need to be close friends to do this, of course, and if it's important to you to do the hooking and landing of your own fish, then you may think it's not for you. But try it some time and enjoy something really different for a change. You may be surprised.

On our trout venture the other week we carried on much the same as usual, with Malcolm spotting and taking the rod in turn, and by about noon we had seven fish including Ken's big one. Then Malcolm spotted a big fish lying under Ken's bank and directed operations from the opposite bank, while I watched from a distance. The fly literally bounced on the trout's nose several times, getting absolutely no reaction at all, and we were all puzzled. It ought at least to have been scared and to have backed away, but it stayed there in its narrow gut between the weeds underneath an overhang of meadowsweet. Ken spent a long time on it but with no result and no movement from the fish whatsoever.

Finally, deciding that what Malcolm could see was not a fish at all, he removed the overhang to see for himself. It was a fish all right, and even the disturbance of removing the trailing foliage didn't disturb it. Something was obviously wrong and Ken finally quietly put the landing net under it and lifted it out.

The fish was a five-pounder, fat and in superb condition—but completely blind!

How long it had been so we've no way of knowing. How it ever found its food will be a mystery, for it was obviously not a fish freshly introduced from the stews.

I wonder how many other anglers have tried for that fish and been puzzled by its complete lack of interest in anything on the end of a line.

Bending the Rules

Some years ago I rented a short stretch of water about nine miles from my home. It stemmed from some watercress beds, widened into a small moat, passed through a grill and disappeared as a mere trickle into the distant woodland. I stocked it with browns and rainbows, which made remarkable progress and provided me with several seasons of good fly fishing. I gave it up reluctantly when I woke up to the fact that the local villagers had cottoned on and were reaping great harvests of *my* fish with worms and bait. Much good it did me to restrict myself to fly only! But that is not the point of this story, which has to do with what is commonly referred to as 'bending the rules'.

I made my own rules on my fishery, and if I decided to bend, or even break, them I was at liberty to do so. Thus it was that, when I took an American friend over to fish, I slipped a couple of slices of bread into my pocket. Bob, my guest, though a superb bait-caster, was not a fly fisher, and a few practice casts could not make him into one, but I thought it would be fitting for him to catch his first-ever trout in England within a few hours of landing at Heathrow. There were ducks on the moat, the owner fed them regularly with bread and ... well, you can see how my mind was working.

Because of the conditions, I had little confidence in fly fishing myself, anyway, and I felt that if I couldn't catch fish that way Bob would be on a licking to nothing, but I insisted he tried at least for an hour. After that hour had resulted in complete failure, I produced the bread and took Bob to where the ducks are usually fed.

There wasn't much to it, of course. The sodden crust lay on the surface for a few minutes and then disappeared with a great slurp any carp would have been proud to have made. Bob tightened, latched on and caught his trout. And that, I thought, was that. He would be tired after his long transatlantic trip and would want to go home to bed. But it was not to be. 'Now, dammit,' he said, 'I'm gonna git me one legit.'

I wouldn't expect anyone to believe it, but, in fact, he did just that. A fluke, maybe, but a fluke that could not have been better timed. I had produced an instant fly fisher with the help of a little rule-breaking and a smile from Lady Luck. And I was most interested to note, on my last visit to Florida, that several fly rods now grace the rack in Bob's tackle room. He will, I know, eventually catch a big tarpon on a fly—an ambition I myself hope to fulfil one day. If and when he does, he will be the first to admit that my little rule-breaking exercise started it all.

Rules, they say, are made for fools, but I am almost tempted to say that some rules are made by fools.

It's probably unfair of me to make such a statement but I can call to mind so many instances of stupid rules that my mind boggles. Are these rules deliberately aimed at preventing the capture of fish? Or are they part and parcel of rules that try to eliminate as many 'cheats' as possible? Are they centred around a true conservation policy with the future in mind? Or are they ancient relics of the past devised when attitudes and fish stocks were different from those of today?

I know one stretch of beautiful sea trout water in the South-West where a fly-only rule is enforced. I have no complaint about the ruling as such, because I fish for sea trout at night. But have you ever seen what effect a thick fly line has upon the occupants of a gin-clear, spate-river pool in bright sunshine? It is devastating. What's more, I'm convinced that a pool disturbed in this way during the daytime does not fish as well at night. And I know that a good worm fisher could fish that self-same pool during the day without scaring the fish and with a reasonable chance of catching one of them.

Had I made the rules for that particular fishing, I would have banned day-time fly fishing. As it is, those who want to fish by day are forced to ruin their own chances by a rule that should never have been. I should, perhaps, mention that I've never been back to that hotel water since and it's possible that the rule has now been changed.

'Upstream dry fly or nymph only' is a rule that is, in itself, commendable. It wouldn't suit me, and so I do not fish waters where it is imposed; but I see the reasons for it, and I am absolutely sure that those who do fish such waters want it no other way. But how do you interpret the rule?

A friend of mine was once fishing such a water and spotted a fish rising in a large eddy, which curled around under his own bank and travelled for some way, as eddies often do, in the opposite direction to the main flow. The trout was headed into the flow of the eddy and my friend cast traditionally upstream to it. He was behaving, in my view, perfectly correctly, but, because he was actually facing downstream of the main flow when he made his cast, he was reported for fishing downstream! As I said before, it's mind-boggling. Again I ask: how do you interpret the rule? And why, I wonder, should someone not be allowed to cast downstream to a fish? Nine times out of ten it's more difficult, anyway. I will concede readily that, if the action is likely to spoil another angler's chances, it is fair enough. But I would have thought that the simple rules of sportsmanship were sufficient.

One of my reasons for going fishing is to try to catch fish, and I'd like to think I can do so without upsetting anyone else and without over-exploitation, but I do not see how it is ever likely to be possible in some circumstances while certain rules are in force.

I have spotted fish in situations where an upstream cast is impossible, and, as I see it, those fish will never be caught. In a year or two they will be dead and wasted.

If it is legal or legitimate to dress a nymph with some fine lead or copper wire to make it sink, cast it upstream to land with a plop and manipulate it in front of a trout that's screwed down on the bottom in ten feet of water, why is it wrong to approach that fish from the upstream end? If it is legitimate to load a nymph with weight in the dressing, why is it wrong to pinch on a shot to achieve the same end?

I've caught many trout (once a six-pounder) by taking the rod apart and fishing with the top joint because that has been the only way of getting the fly over them. I've caught fish with the leader knot still in the rod rings for the same reason.

I once caught a deep-lying trout from a fast run by pinching on to the dropper a piece of clay the weight of which took the amber nymph on the point down quickly. Lord knows if in doing so I broke or bent the rules past the point of forgiveness, but I've never made any secret about it. And my conscience is clear enough, otherwise I'd never have written this.

Trends

I never was a very enthusiastic early-season trout fisher, and while it is always a temptation to visit those waters which have opening dates in March and April, I am usually pulled up smartly by memories of seasons past. Trout fishing, to me, is something to be practised in pleasant conditions. Warm days, buzzing insects and the smell of approaching summer are what really stir me to dig out my fly tackle each year.

Who could have relished fly fishing after looking out of the window, as I did, at a veritable blizzard on the first invitation day of 1979? Not I. Some did and some profess to have enjoyed it, but I have my doubts about them all. Fly fishing for trout in a snowstorm? It is surely all wrong.

One of my closest friends, who scorns my coarse fishing, especially winter pike fishing, tells me every season that the nice thing about fly fishing for trout is that it is practised at the best time of year. I'll agree that it probably *was once*, but after years of fighting winds and waves on exposed reservoirs in April, I have decided that he must be made of better stuff.

The time for trout fishing in my book is after 1 May. Even then conditions *can* be atrocious, but at least the chances of gales, snow, hail and heavy downpours are reduced. Besides which, I am convinced that fish are in better condition then. I recall the April day when waves, some two feet high, were breaking on the banks of the local reservoir. All but one lone stalwart had retired to the local for something sustaining, and I joined them.

'I got wet outside,' said one, 'now, dammit, I'll get wet inside.' My feelings exactly, except that I had not even bothered to take my rod out of its bag. The sight of the lone survivor, standing *back* to the water, punching line out *with* the wind on his forward cast and releasing it on to the water with his back cast looked like work to me, and I decided I could do that any time.

Don't misunderstand me. The skill necessary to keep up that kind of fishing for long is something I do not have. I appreciate it in others and I admire their persistence but it is something

I do not enjoy. As far as I am concerned, fishing *has* to be enjoyed, and the catching of limits, though very satisfying, is not essential for my own pleasure.

I shall never have the great casting skills of those who bank-fish big exposed reservoirs regularly. There was a time when I could just about hold my own, but now an old shoulder injury prevents my doing much false-casting and double-hauling. I can never achieve great success out of sheer casting ability and in recent years I have had to rely upon a certain amount of craft. I am no great shakes at entomology, either, though I have a brother who ties superb flies, and sometimes I myself dream up a pattern that succeeds.

Most of my pleasure comes from drifting in a boat, or bank-stalking to observe what goes on in the water. Not, I hasten to add, with thoughts in mind of 'matching the hatch' or anything as advanced as that. It really matters little to me what is happening on the surface, except that I look for signs of fish.

I can hardly tell one fly from another and I doubt if I'll ever get 'into' fly recognition now. I am the first to admit that there are many occasions when the ability to fish with an exact or near-imitation of whatever the trout are eating is an advantage. But I am sure that there are just as many when a completely dissimilar fly will succeed.

A few years ago I fished at Little Tring Reservoir with some eight other anglers. The water literally boiled with rising fish and word went round that the trout were 'on the black buzzer'.

As far as I can remember, most of the anglers present put up buzzer patterns and took their limits of four fish each. I stayed with a black-and-white lure fly—an Integration—and took my limit scraping the bottom. There are often just as many trout feeding below as there are up above when a rise is taking place. Or is that really the case?

Rainbows are aggressive and will sometimes turn from steady, rhythmic, surface-feeding behaviour to strike at what appears to be a tiny intruder. I have seen this at close range and I have watched a surface-feeding fish follow a loaded bucktail six feet down to the bottom and take it as it was speeding back to the rod.

I recall a day on the Test when an unusually busy mayfly hatch was taking place, and, being completely without anything looking the slightest bit like a mayfly, I continued fishing with a favourite loaded shrimp pattern. I took my limit without any trouble at all and proved, at least to my own satisfaction, that not *every* trout in the river was on the mayfly. On two occasions I sat over fish that were rising precisely, methodically and regularly. Both actually followed my loaded shrimp downstream before taking it.

I doubt very much if a wild brown trout could be so fooled, but few of us are ever likely to be involved regularly in the pursuit of wild brown trout. Today, however, because of the excellent trout conservation policies carried out by commercial undertakings, we have more trout and more trout fishermen than at any other time in our history. The fact that the trout are aggressive rainbows and not native fish has brought about a change in our tackle and our approach to fly fishing. Who, twenty years ago, would have considered casting a trout fly forty yards? Who would have thought of fly fishing in November? And where will it end? Shall we soon have a year-long season for rainbows?

Since they do not spawn naturally (with one or two exceptions) in this country, they are hardly entitled to a close season and the time will come, I'm sure, when sterile hybrids are introduced to exclusive waters for year-round fishing.

I find it odd that our own water authorities insist on giving alien rainbows a close season, while those in the far west of America, where rainbows do spawn naturally, impose no restrictions of season, bait, or method. An old friend of mine out there once told me that 'if you can catch 'em, they're in season'. He meant by that, of course, that the long winter imposed a natural close season. But anyone who cares to do so is at liberty to fish through the ice with jig, fly or bait.

I wish our own laws could be as liberally interpreted. Bait fishing for trout need not involve mass slaughter as so many seem to think. It would be nice, in hopeless conditions, to be allowed to sit and watch a float and not have to flail away with tackle that makes fishing hard work.

Along with many others, I have worm-fished for rainbows in the American West with no feelings of guilt, and certainly without bringing about any deterioration in the fishing. In fact, method is of little importance when strict bag limits are enforced.

I'd enjoy my trout fishing here a lot more if I could use methods to suit conditions, and I still live in hope that the time *will* come when trout fishing on public waters does not begin and end with fly-only rulings.

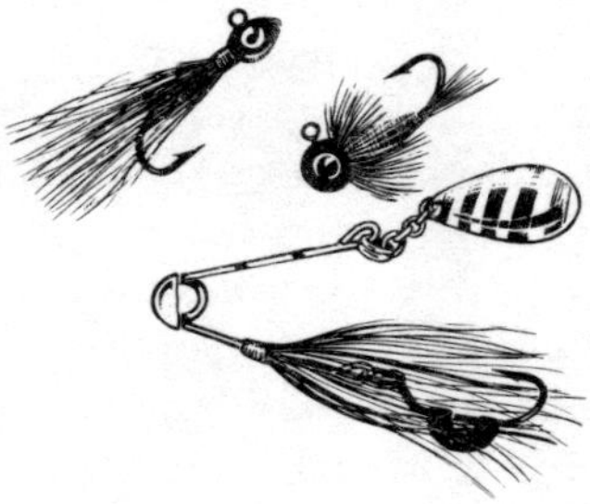

The Hook-Shedders

The day was warm and overcast. My brother Ken and I were walking slowly upstream on opposite banks of the narrow river trying to locate fish for each other, as we often do, but we had had very little success so far.

I think we both spotted the big brown together and we stopped dead in our tracks. The fish was holding steadily in the current above a bare patch of gravel and, as we watched, it dived nose first into the patch and began digging into the bottom. After a few seconds it retired to its holding place, remained there briefly and then repeated the procedure, releasing clouds of silty sand as it did so.

'That,' said Ken, 'is the first time I've ever seen a trout feeding like a carp!' And I agreed. It was strange behaviour for a trout and, as its diggings appeared to become more and more frantic as time went by, we tried to figure out what was so special about that particular gravel patch. We cast over the fish several times while it rested at mid-water level, but it showed no interest whatsoever in anything we were able to offer, and we were puzzled. Finally it dawned upon us that this fish was not feeding at all. It was trying desperately to rid itself of a small fly and a length of nylon leader by rubbing its mouth on the hard bottom. It was persistent,

I'll say that for it, and we both spent a long time watching it (I nearly said 'wasted a lot of time', but that would have been wrong), almost willing it to succeed.

It was probably an hour before it gave up trying and set out on a long and almost desperate run upstream. It was obviously irritated, though not seriously distressed, but as it cruised up and down between the two bridges it seemed to transfer its irritation to several other hitherto unseen trout causing them to leave their lies and behave in similar fashion.

For a time, great bow waves showed here and there as fish after fish, thoroughly unsettled, made runs up and down the beat before quietly returning to shelter. It didn't improve the fishing but it certainly served to illustrate how one disturbed fish can affect the behaviour of others.

Several times after that, we spotted the big brown still scraping away at the gravel patch and towards late afternoon we located it again, quiet and finally rid of the hook that had been causing all the trouble. There was a raw spot on its lower jaw where it had obviously rubbed away part of the gristle in the process. Amazingly enough, it began to feed about an hour afterwards, but we weren't smart enough to catch it then, and in a way I was rather glad—I reckon it deserved a break.

I really find it hard to understand why some anglers persist in fishing for big trout in the confines of a narrow overgrown river with tackle that is obviously inadequate. These fish have to be held hard and there's no way you can hold a big trout on a 2-pound point in these circumstances. Some argue that it is the only way to induce a rise or to fool a fish into taking, but I have never found it necessary to fish finer than 4-pound there. I've lost fish, it's true, but I can honestly say that I do not recall such a loss ever being through line breakage.

I've had hooks pull out and I've had them straighten. I've had the odd one or two break at the barb because I've allowed them to become rusty by sticking them into a wet hat and forgetting them, but I've no recollection of leaving hooks and lengths of nylon in the fish of that water. In trees, yes, many times—but not in fish.

Leaving aside the emotional aspect of what it does to the fish itself, I think it's worth bearing in mind what effect a lost fish can have on other people's fishing. Fish that might otherwise be free feeders become restless and neurotic when another, obviously disturbed, fish passes among them, and they'll only calm down in their own good time. There's no way you can make them forget or revert to normal behaviour.

The disturbance is, of course, only temporary and I'd hazard that in a couple of days most fish are able to rid themselves of hooks. I've heard tell of fish being caught with several flies already in their mouths, but I haven't seen it myself, and I can only assume that some hooks or flies embed themselves in spots that do not irritate or inconvenience their 'hosts'.

When you consider the numbers of fish that are lost all over the country—and I'm including coarse fish here, of course—it's quite astonishing how few of us ever catch fish carrying hooks. I've caught pike with snaps and trebles in them as well as small hooks obviously intended for roach, but with few exceptions they did not give the appearance of having been hooked long. It's my belief that most fish are remarkably capable of ridding themselves of hooks, but I haven't the faintest idea how it's done.

There was a time when I used to worry about removing the hooks from a badly hooked pike but now I treat each situation as an individual case, and I'm convinced that there are times when it's better to return a fish with the hooks still in. Sometimes, in spite of great care and proper equipment, a pike that undergoes a lengthy, bankside, hook-removal operation is worse off than one that's returned quickly with the hooks trimmed down and left inside.

I'll never forget the story Ian Howcroft told many years ago about the pike he 'killed' and took home because it was too badly hooked to return. Despite a knock on the head and a long journey, the fish was still alive when he arrived and so he put it in the bath and left it to take its chance.

It revived and began swimming around shortly afterwards and a few hours later both the trebles and wire trace were no longer in its throat but wrapped around the bath plug chain! I've always felt it a great pity that the whole operation wasn't filmed for posterity.

Back in the 1950s I hooked a carp on a soft-boiled potato and a No. 6 treble, and because all points were well embedded deep at the back of its throat I bit the line through and put the fish in a big keepnet. It was pitch dark and I thought I'd do the fish less harm if I worked on it by daylight. At the crack of dawn I took the fish out of the net, intending to remove the hook, but it was no longer there. It was not in the keepnet either, and there were no red marks or signs on the fish of it ever having been there. And unless someone else sneaked along and swapped my fish for another sixteen-pounder, I cannot think what happened to that hook. I can only assume that the fish somehow managed to remove it and swallow it along with the foot or so of 11-pound nylon to which it was attached!

It is said that both chub and tench are capable of transferring hooks to weed and rush stems while still attached to a rod and line, but while I *have* occasionally ended up playing a lily stem, I can't convince myself that the changeover was intentional!

Some say that a chub can fill its mouth with weed to such an extent that the hook is forced out, but whenever I've hooked a fish, chub, tench, carp, or whatever, in soft weed I've usually found they've given up trying almost at once and that a steady pressure brings them (and half the weed-bed too) into the bank. Occasionally the pressure applied is such that the hook pulls free, and there *have* been times when I've thought the fish was still there but found it very much missing when the weed reached the net. I'm of the opinion, however, that a fish buried in soft weed is capable of doing precious little to help itself, and there have been times when I've been glad to see a big trout bury itself in soft weed upstream—fish that I've been fairly sure I'd have lost otherwise.

Ted Andrews was telling me recently that he hooked a Stour roach of about twelve ounces in the gristly part of the jaw and that he simply could not get it out. To save time he put the fish in the keepnet and tied on a fresh hook in order to make the best of the last half-hour or so while the fish were 'on'. When the time came to release the roach, the hook had disappeared completely.

Here is a case where there was no available leverage and no facilities for a direct pull or tangle, and yet the hook had somehow or other been shifted.

Is it done by muscle contraction or by magic? Perhaps we'll never know, but it's something to puzzle over, and it might help ease our consciences when we lose the odd fish through line breakage.

By the way, Ken caught the trout a week later. It was fat and full of fight and, apart from a raw lip, none the worse for having been hooked.

Action Shots

There were only a couple of days to go before the coarse fishing season opened and thoughts of trout were furthest from my mind. All I could think of were the chances of success or otherwise of the prebaiting programme I'd been carrying out for the past few weeks. I'd seen activity in the swims I'd prepared, and while the fish present all appeared to be small, I regarded them as a good sign. Small fish often serve to attract bigger ones.

Then I had my arm twisted to go trout fishing.

'You owe me a day on the stream,' said my friend Al Pond, 'so what about it?'

It was true. I'd promised him, weeks ago, that we would go, and now he was holding me to it.

It was four-thirty in the morning when he arrived at my door. He was half an hour late but, knowing Al, I had anticipated this, so we got away in good time.

It's really a two-hour trip to the water but Al made it in just over an hour and a half and we were fishing by six-thirty.

Normally the water is clear, the trout are easily seen and just as easily scared, but on this morning the light was bad and the stream was running a little coloured. We saw no fish, though I imagine we scared plenty that saw us.

By nine o'clock we'd taken nothing and so we stopped for breakfast on the bridge. Suddenly the water came alive. Fish began to rise and splash all over, and big rings appeared along the whole length of the stream.

We promptly forgot breakfast!

I'm no entomologist, but I didn't need to be to see what all the fuss was about. Black flies were in evidence everywhere and they looked to me to be about the biggest black gnats I'd ever seen. I thought at first that they were hawthorns, but that little 'undercarriage', peculiar to the hawthorn, was missing. Not that it would have made any difference anyway. On that particular day any black-hackled fly would have served to catch fish, as we quickly learned. At one stage we both had fish on at the same time, and within less than an hour we had taken five nice rainbows.

The limit for that water is eight fish and at that point we stopped fishing and took stock of the situation.

Al is a photographer and he, naturally, wanted to make the most of this opportunity to take some action shots, so he left the rest of the fishing to me.

I spotted a fish rising upstream and crept up to it, keeping out of sight as well as I could, expecting to see Al creeping up behind me. When I looked back, however, I saw him standing, with three cameras slung round his neck, in the middle of the stream well downstream of where the fish was rising.

'Catch it,' he said, 'then, if it belts off downstream towards me, hold it hard and see if it jumps.'

Charming! It reminded me of the time when I was playing a big pike for the TV cameras and a frogman's head appeared suddenly by the side of the boat and a voice said, 'I say, can you let it do that again—I don't think I quite got it.'

Trying to catch a fish to order is bad enough. Trying to control its behaviour after you've hooked it is, in my view, asking too much. But luck was with us. The fish took immediately and hared off downstream towards Al. I held it as hard as I dared and it leapt and leapt and leapt again while Al feverishly clicked away at his shutters. It was all good fun and we tried the same tactics with two more fish later, but we didn't get quite the same results.

That was our limit, of course, and though, I suppose, we could have fished on and returned any others we caught, we both felt that enough was enough. I have never agreed with returning trout in these circumstances. Other people have to fish the water and I believe that it is better, on a well-stocked fishery, to take a limit and quit.

Where the numbers of wild fish are limited, there is a case for returning fish in order to ensure that future stocks are maintained, but on this water it is neither necessary nor advisable.

I had put the fish on my American stringer and hung them in the water as we caught them. In the cold stream they remained fresh and moist, which is how they should be. There is no more depressing sight, to my mind, than a fine fat trout that has dried and shrivelled up in the summer sun. Nor is there anything more repulsive than a pile of sticky trout that have been wrapped in a plastic bag and chucked into the hot boot of a car.

Why, I wonder, do people treat fish this way? Why, after working hard to catch fish in good condition, do they allow them to deteriorate on the way home? Why, when fish have to be cleaned eventually, do they take them home with the guts still inside?

Any trout I take are deep-frozen for some future occasion and I like to ensure that they go into the freezer fresh. On this day, as always, I put ours in the cooler box. I carry one with me all through the summer months, whether I am coarse fishing, salmon fishing or trout fishing. In fact, I often carry more than one.

They're easily made out of boxes lined with polystyrene and they serve to protect bait and food as well as fish. Plastic bottles or some bait-boxes filled with ice will last a whole weekend and, besides acting as a mini-fridge, they provide ice-cold water for drinks as well.

That's something I learned to appreciate on my American trips. I also acquired the habit of gutting and cleaning my fish at the water's edge, and ensuring that, even in the hottest of weather, my catch stays fresh until I get home. The trout I catch are not left to smell and attract flies in a car boot, because I believe they're worthy of a better end than that.

Up a Tree

'Pike don't grow on trees,' said my brother Ken. 'What are you doing up there?'

I was up a tree retrieving a rather expensive plug that I couldn't get to any other way, and it was proving to be a decidedly dangerous occupation. All right for ten-year-olds—but not for me. However, I did retrieve my plug and, having overcome my initial fear of the height (I was twelve feet up in the air at least), I lay across the big willow branch and looked down into the water. After all, it wasn't the first time I'd been up a tree and I hope it won't be the last.

And by that I do not necessarily mean in order to retrieve plugs or other tackle. I've been up trees for a good many other reasons, not the least of which is fish spotting. On the day in question I saw only one fish under that tree; a big rudd which showed itself briefly and drifted back into the shadows again. I may or may not have located a shoal of big rudd, but at least I have a spot marked to try next time I visit the water.

Yes, you can learn a lot from climbing trees, and if you've enough courage and a good friend you can hook fish from them too. Ask Pat Russel. He once went carp fishing and arrived an hour or so before his companion Pete Thomas. When Pete arrived, Pat was halfway up a willow tree with a carp, beaten, at the end of his line, and was completely powerless to land it. Good job Pete arrived when he did!

Pat's like me, and a good many others too, in that he worries about getting the fish on the hook first, and only then worries about landing it. It isn't always wise to do so, but if you see an opportunity, it's very difficult to resist it. And sometimes the only means of getting a bait to a fish is by climbing a tree first.

I remember once spotting a big trout under an overhang. I couldn't cast to it at all but I could see it well and I knew it was feeding. So I climbed a nearby tree, poked the fly rod through the branches and dangled a nymph into the water. It was no good; it was swept away much too quickly—so I cheated a little. I pinched a shot on the leader above the nymph and let it sink in front of the fish. After a second or two I raised it slowly by pulling on the line, and I watched the trout move and take—what the late Oliver Kite, the master nymph fisher, would have called an induced take, though I doubt if he would have approved!

Well *I* approved! And I thought I'd done very well to hook that fish at all. There was no other way of doing it as far as I could see, but at that stage my troubles were only just beginning. If you think it's easy trying to control a three-pound fish from up a tree with the reel screaming blue murder and the trout trying to jump the bridge thirty yards upstream, you're mistaken. It isn't, and you've got to have a little luck on your side to help compensate. Fortunately, I had some. I managed to climb down the tree and play the fish through the branches until a friend came along and netted it. We had several other fish that day but none were more deserved than that one!

And talking of trout fishing from a tree reminds me of an episode which Vic Evans and I enjoyed one summer, which I feel is well worth recording. In fact it's a great pity it couldn't have been *tape* recorded!

We were on opposite sides of a very small stream, Vic and I, and I spotted a huge trout under his bank. I climbed a tree on my side and looked down on the fish while Vic tried to fish for it from well back on the opposite bank. He was lying on his belly with his rod tip poking out over the water, and trying to follow my instructions as to where to place his weighted nymph. It was a light-coloured nymph, easy to see in the water and from my vantage-point up the tree I could see the fish's every reaction. I don't know how Vic felt, but I was absolutely fascinated.

I gave a running commentary which went something like this.

'No, you've drifted past him, pull back slowly and drop in a little higher upstream. That's it! He's seen it—he's moving to it! No, he's moved away. Give it a little tweak—and another—and another. That's it. *Leave* it! Now he's interested, his fins are going. He's moved over to it, he's going to take. . . . No, he's backed away. Have another cast. No, you're too far out, come in a bit closer to your bank. That's it! It's right in front of him. He's watching it, he's *got* it! No, he's spat it out. Try again. That's it. That's it. Leave it. It's actually touching his gill cover. Give it a tiny, tiny tweak. No, too much, you've pulled it too far and it's gone on downstream!'

This sort of thing went on for over thirty minutes, and I could have stuck it all day I was so enthralled. But Vic, after all, is only made of flesh and blood. You'd have to be super-human to stand more than half an hour of that without simply *having* to try and *see* what was going on. In the end he cracked. He hurled his rod from him, put his cheek to the grass and pounded the ground with his fists.

'I can't stand it,' he groaned. 'I can't stand it!'

So we left that fish, and as far as I know, it's still there for the catching. Perhaps Vic will have recovered enough by next year to have another go at it, but I fear he's not been the same man since. That sort of thing can have a telling effect on a man!

I know it only too well, for I have been on the receiving end myself many times.

Dick Walker and I spent part of one season doing something similar with a shoal of big barbel. That was pretty nerve-racking, believe me.

When you see a barbel that could be twenty pounds nosing your partner's bait or looking at it with interest; or alternatively, if it's *your* bait and your partner is telling you that you are within a millimetre of hooking a record fish, it can be trying, to say the least. Those fish were among the most cussed I have ever encountered and, in spite of all that has been said to the contrary, they have proved quite impossible to catch so far.

Oh, we caught the small ones and some of the medium-sized ones years ago. Others have taken them since, but they still haven't taken the big ones. They're still impossible, in my book—at least for the time being.

Perhaps next time one or other of us is up the tree watching them, they'll be more co-operative, but they'll provide their share of thrills even if they aren't.

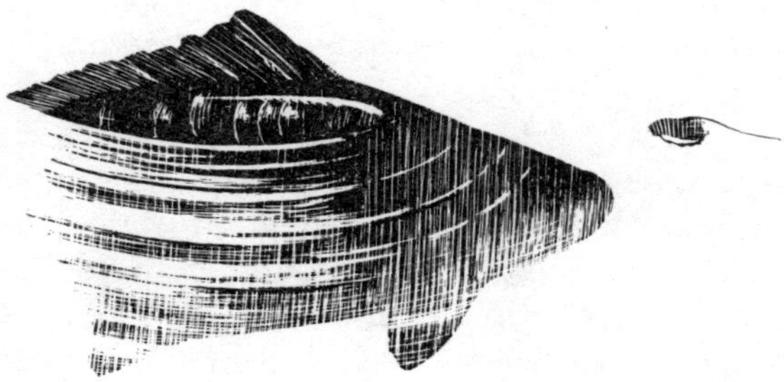

Lucky Pike

Of all the kinds of fishing I practise, pike fishing has always appeared to me to be the one involving the biggest slice of luck. I do not regard the catching of a big pike very highly in terms of angling skill and it always amuses me when I'm asked (by obvious non-anglers) to tell of my biggest pike. These good people never ask me about my biggest roach or chub or barbel because for some reason they have a much higher regard for the mysterious and savage pike. They refer to it as the freshwater shark; they have heard countless legends regarding its size, appetite and great strength, and there is, I suppose, a romantic aspect to their question.

Those non-anglers can be forgiven for their wrong impressions, but there really is no earthly reason for the novice angler to be apprehensive about pike fishing. Pike are just fish. They respond to fishing methods, techniques and baits just like any other species. And if the truth be told, they're a whole lot easier, in the main, to catch than most.

Undoubtedly, there are difficult waters and waters holding too few pike to make fishing for them a worthwhile proposition, but where the population is reasonable, the novice, with a little luck, stands just as much chance of hooking into a big fish as the topmost expert. There are, of course, such things as casting ability and fish handling to be considered, but it's surprising how naturally these skills are acquired in the course of a few outings.

There are many pike-fishing situations demanding special techniques if the absolute maximum of success is to be achieved, but even those situations very often respond to the simplest tackle and a relaxed approach. You can, if you're not careful, make a very simple style of fishing more complicated than it need be. And, in view of the fact that, generally speaking, there's very little opportunity of being selective regarding the size of pike you catch, the chances of a really big fish are ever present. In fact, I believe that, of all our coarse fish species, the pike offers the novice the best chance of a real specimen. One has only to read the angling reports from week to week to learn of yet another twenty-pounder falling to a complete novice on his first-ever attempt.

So why do many coarse fishers of limited experience resist the urge to go piking in winter? Why do they claim complete indifference to pike until they have the good fortune to latch into a big one? (Believe me, it's a very different story then!)

I have no desire to try to convert the anglers who are genuinely uninterested, but I would like to try and convince those who have refrained largely through lack of know-how and/or confidence, that pike fishing is fun, and that no special qualifications are required.

The one essential, of course, is a water known to hold pike. It's true enough that there are very few waters completely devoid of pike, but unless they are known to be present in numbers, pike fishing can be a waste of time.

For the most part, and whether the River Authority's by-laws enforce it or not, pike fishing does not normally begin until October. It's a strange relic of bygone days when iron-hard banks and blizzards were reputed to be ideal pike-fishing conditions. No one seems to know why anglers thought that way, but unless the pike's habits have changed considerably in the last fifty years there could have been very little truth in the theory. Pike have been caught in such conditions, naturally. I have caught them myself after breaking holes in the ice, but I'm happier fishing in less rigorous conditions and I usually catch more pike after a thaw than after a freeze.

Pike waters with good reputations are generally well known to most local club anglers and there should be no difficulty in choosing a water. If local knowledge is not available, however, one of the safest and surest ways of locating pike is to go roach fishing! Continued activity, feeding, attracting and lifting out roach often has the effect of bringing a pike (or several pike) into the area. Its presence is indicated either by a complete cessation of bites or an attack on a hooked and struggling roach.

And of course, there are days when a water appears to be alive with striking pike. It happens mostly in summer and occasionally on mild autumn days. When it does it is no indication that the pike are necessarily bent on suicide or that hookbaits will be taken with wild abandon, but it *does* give an idea of the numbers of pike present and whether or not they are worth pursuing.

Having decided on the water to be fished, by one means or another, it now remains for the bait, lure or whatever, to be presented in a manner acceptable to the pike. And here's the problem.

There are so many methods, so many baits, so many outfits, so many presentations, that the beginner, if he allows himself to be blinded by science, will be more confused than ever.

But a start has to be made, and the simplest start, as I see it, is to put a bait out where it will stay put and await the pike's pleasure. Put it out where it can be seen or located by the pike, put it out on tackle that will hold a pike when hooked, and then leave well alone.

It's possible to put out a livebait on snap tackle to fulfil all these requirements, but I do not believe it is necessary or even advisable (in view of the ever increasing numbers of 'antis' in our midst) to stick hooks into live fish and let them swim around till they die. I believe that a dead roach, rudd, dace, herring, sprat, mackerel or any other similar-sized fish will, in the long run, attract and account for just as many pike as a tethered livebait. There may be waters where livebaits outfish deadbaits, but there are just as many where the reverse is true.

A dead fish, lying on the bottom of a lake, in an area reasonably free from weed, will generally cause little suspicion on the pike's part. It's a natural presentation. It requires little in the way of ironmongery, and because a pike does not have to react violently in order to pick up a dead fish, bites are likely to be confident. There are complications at times because fishing pressure and heavy pre-baiting can cause pike to react in different ways.

Pike that have been caught on deadbaits and returned several times often tend to be a bit wild in their mode of attack. They will occasionally pick up the bait, hold it lightly, and swim off with it at high speed, before either accepting it or rejecting it completely. It's difficult to advise on when to strike such runs. One can only imagine that the pike itself has allowed its hunger to overcome its natural caution, and, having made the decision, behaves in a manner somewhat akin to panic.

I have tried hitting these runs at every stage of the game from the initial twitch on the line to the final resting place sixty or more yards away. I've made contact at every stage of the game too, but I've made *more* contacts by waiting for the first run to stop and the second to commence. Sometimes (though rarely, I find) long waits result in gorged baits, but more often than not these 'streaker' runs end up with the pike barely hooked.

Baits that are picked up and swallowed on the spot are those that present the biggest problems, and need the closest attention. Where pre-baiting has presented all the pike with easily acquired food in quantities that do away with the need for competition, the pike run as we know it no longer exists. Loose fish are shovelled up and swallowed, so are the hookbaits. And the almost essential, gory bankside operation to remove the hooks must be the number one reason to ban heavy pre-baiting with dead fish.

These things happen with deadbaits and no one can really lay down any hard-and-fast rules about how long to let the pike run continue. Nor can anyone define what steps are necessary to ensure that gorging or complete bait rejection does not take place. These decisions have to be made with due regard to the pattern of the pike's behaviour from water to water, but my own thoughts on the subject are very uncomplicated.

If a pike is prepared to pick up a deadbait and set off on a long steady run before stopping, turning and pouching it, I will let it do so. In the main, I feel my chances of setting the hooks and seeing the fish on the bank are greatly increased if the pike behaves in this rather traditional manner.

If, after a long run, the bait is rejected and the bite does not develop further, I think in terms of striking sooner. If, after a traditional run or an unnoticeable twitch, I find the bait has been gorged, I try to arrange for it not to happen again and I speed my strike accordingly. One gorged bait or one rejected bait, however, does not mean that all ensuing bites will end up the same way, and it is only after a period of trial and error that the pattern, if any, will be noted.

These are but a few of the problems likely to be encountered throughout a season of deadbaiting for pike. They are, for the most part, moral and not technical problems, but there are technical answers to some of the moral problems.

Single-hook rigs can be devised which, if swallowed, will do no harm to the pike if left where they are. The pike's digestive juices are well capable of eroding away a hook or a piece of single-strand wire, and the novice need feel no guilt about leaving in swallowed hooks. Better to return a pike with the hook snipped off close, than to dig away with disgorgers and gags to save a few pence or in the mistaken belief that the fish will die if the hooks are left in. Unless the gills are badly damaged (and disgorgers, gags and pliers often do more damage than hooks in this delicate area), gut-hooked pike only come to serious harm when the hooks are ripped out.

So, moral problems aside, what can the novice or first-time pike fisher do to be reasonably sure of success? The answer, I'm sure, is to spend his time legering deadbaits in a water known to hold a good head of pike.

It doesn't really matter too much about rods. A flimsy tip-actioned roach rod will not do, but a medium-actioned carp or barbel rod will suffice at a push. Line strength can be anything from 8- to 20-pound test and the conditions and size of fish expected will decide this. The choice is yours.

A single-strand wire hook-mount incorporating one or more hooks (singles or trebles, depending on your conscience) attached to the reel line with a swivel and carrying an appropriate bait hooked in the manner of your choice is the only terminal tackle required. No leads are needed—they are in fact inadvisable.

After casting, the bait is allowed to sink under its own weight, the rod is put in rests, the bale arm of the reel is left open and the waiting game begins. It's not in any way complicated.

What you do with your in-between time is up to you. You *could* spend it watching the scenery or drinking coffee, but if you're wise you'll start roach fishing. It will keep you busy *and* improve your chances.

A Day of Solitude

I am probably too involved with practicalities ever to be called a sentimentalist, but there are times when I become a little that way inclined. It has all to do with fishing, of course, and these little pangs of sentiment always come when I am alone at the water. As I have to fish when opportunities occur, I cannot always fit in with other people's plans, which often means that I have to fish alone or not at all. I do not particularly enjoy being on my own—indeed, I feel that an experience shared with someone else is very often an improved experience—but I have to admit that there have been many times in the past when my catches have been the better for it.

I long ago decided that the coach outing, and all that went with it, was not for me. I have felt in the past that part of going fishing meant doing my best to catch fish and I never found that possible when I had to compete with another thirty anglers for a few feet of bank space. Perhaps that is why I never became a match angler—I found it hard enough to beat the fish without the added problems of a coachload of fishermen. I am not against coach parties: if thousands of anglers every week are prepared to settle for ten yards of bank each, that must leave a lot more space available for those who like room to move—and I am all for that, especially as so many people obviously enjoy that kind of fishing.

My ideal is to fish with one or two close companions and to plan, somehow, to catch fish between us. I believe it is really enjoyable to work together with a certain objective in mind and for success to come through team-work. It does not matter a scrap then who catches the fish. It is just nice to be able to say that we caught what we set out to catch.

But it is not always possible to do things that way and when I have to fish alone I am conscious that something is missing. I notice it especially when I am fishing a water which, in the past, has been the scene of many hours of concentrated team-work and co-operation.

One recent autumn I had an afternoon to spare, so I took some deep frozen small rudd and a box of plugs down to what was once one of my favourite haunts—the Warrells Lake.

I believe here I learned more about general fishing from just one corner of that beautiful lake than from any other water I have fished, and I think I've spent more happy hours in and around the derelict tea-house on the bank than anywhere else in the world. It was nice to be back there again after a long absence, and although I had really intended to spend my time spinning with deadbaits and plugs, it seemed more fitting when I arrived to settle down and leger, for it was here, in this very spot, that the first steps in developing legered deadbait techniques were taken in the early 1950s.

Someone before me had left a forked stick in the bank and it seemed fitting, too, that I should make use of it after I had cast out my deadbait. Back in 1951 Joe Taylor had made use of a similar forked stick and had started us on a completely new train of thought. For reasons only known to himself he had dropped his rod into one of the many such 'rests' present while he lit his cigarette, and in the brief moment it took to do so, a pike had picked up his bait from the bottom. That was the start of an exciting new venture and during the next few years we worked on it until we had proved a number of points beyond doubt.

I was reminded of all this as I sat in the October sunshine and I recalled some of the great days we had there.

We had never had any twenty-pounders but we did get a lot of fish in the double-figure bracket and it was not at all unusual to catch twenty pike in the course of a short autumn day. But there was much more to it than that. There were the fires we used to light and sit around when the weather was really foul. We had one special area where we were allowed to burn refuse and brew tea for working parties and competitions during the winter. No one minded if we made use of those facilities when we were fishing 'free-lance', and I remember many times when our herring baits ended up by being impaled on pike gags and toasted over the embers.

Those were happy days, but there were others days too, and nights.

Sometimes we would fish the night through, hoping to catch carp. Other times we would sleep in deckchairs or on piles of rushes after baiting down overnight for the tench fishing next morning. What nights they were! Full of hope, excitement, frustration, mystery. Each one was different, each one held new promise, but, despite the great beauty of the lake by day, there was a certain eeriness about it at night.

I would never have fished there alone, and I can remember being more than a little scared even with close friends present. Close friends like Eric Bailey, a bailiff who was as keen to catch carp as we were, and who often beat us to the water on Friday nights. Out of the blackness would come his phoney Al Read accent, and his sinister 'Are you glad you coom?' would never fail to scare us.

I will never know how many potatoes Eric boiled up in his old copper to pre-bait for our carp-fishing sessions, but I know he used to buy them by the hundredweight. Had we caught as many pounds of carp as Eric bought potatoes we might have made history. It never really clicked for us, but it certainly taught us how to fish at night. The summerhouse corner was where we learned how to handle tackle and fish in the darkness. We learned the hard way, but we learned about lots of other things besides fishing. Like the night I took a great swig of Tizer and found out it was methylated spirits! It was in a Tizer bottle and in the darkness it looked like Tizer. That is something you never do twice. I spent a ghastly night with a burned-out throat before I could get to hospital for treatment next day.

These were my October memories on that day and now in the October of my life I am glad to have experienced them. What did I care who won the last big Open Championship, or the National? What did I care about the barbel record or who caught last season's biggest pike? I had caught a big barbel *and* a big pike. I had caught big other fish too and I might yet do so again —but it wasn't important any more....

I was suddenly aware of the fact that loops of line were falling off the end of my reel spool. They were peeling off so slowly that I was sure it was just a light breeze or surface drift causing it. My line was running directly out from the rod tip, however, and I realised that something on the other end was slowly pulling at it. I watched, fascinated, not knowing quite what to do. The pike at the Warrells were notably awkward creatures. Strike too quickly, and they would be gone. Leave things too long, and the hooks would be gorged.

I picked up the rod, drew in slack line with my fingers and felt-out the situation. The fish was still there and I struck firmly into what felt like solid rock.

There were no acrobatics, no streaking runs and no moments of doubt. The pike fought strongly, boring deep but never really testing my tackle.

It came slowly towards the tea-house corner and surfaced apparently quite beaten. It was much bigger than I had expected, and since I had no gaff I drew it towards my outstretched left hand, intending to grip it behind the gill cover as I did with smaller fish. At this moment the pike came to life and I returned to the upright, half-drowned with spray, trying desperately to keep in touch with this totally transformed creature.

Seconds earlier it had been coming in like a lamb. Now, with its temper fully roused, it was stripping off line and behaving like a demented tiger. It could not last, of course, and when this last despairing attempt at escape was foiled, it came to my open hand without resisting. I dropped the rod, grasped the fish with both hands in a wild stranglehold, and hauled it up the bank. As I did so the hooks pulled clear.

It weighed, as near as I could tell on my neglected spring balance, sixteen pounds. It was the biggest pike I had ever taken from the Warrells and probably one of the biggest on record from that lake.

By record standards it was puny and, compared with the size of fish caught in the adjoining Sawmills Lake, it was not worthy of note, but it had been a part of my day and I was pleased.

As I packed up my tackle, I was very conscious of the fact that company would have been out of place on that particular afternoon. It was meant to be a day of solitude—too precious to be shared with anyone else.

And I am sure the moorhen that turned up to share my sandwiches agreed with me.

Tantalisers

The little jigs I first brought back from America in 1967, and again almost every year since then, have, over the years, proved remarkably effective for a number of different fish. There have been times when I have looked upon them as little short of magic, but for the life of me I do not know why!

They are simply loaded hooks with offset eyes and wisps of feather, hair or plastic worm attachments. I cannot imagine what the fish take them for, but it is sufficient, I suppose, that they do. To date, these little creations have accounted for dace, chub, pike, grayling, rudd and perch, and small zander. The strange thing about that, obviously, is the fact that not all of those species are recognised as predatory. For these jigs are designed essentially to deal with predators, so it has been somewhat of a surprise to me to find that other fish occasionally accept them readily. I realise, of course, that all fish are, to some extent, predatory. Big rudd eat very immature rudd fry and even bream have been known to take minnows, but this does not necessarily mean that small fish are always an essential part of their diet.

The jig does not resemble a small fish in any way, but it appears to be alive in the water when it is worked correctly. Just as the heavy stainless-steel jig used by the sea angler so effectively for cod has to be kept on the move, so does the little American fresh-water jig have to be worked continually. It is not enough to cast and retrieve automatically and leave it at that, nor is it often of any use allowing the jig to lie at rest, though there have been exceptions. The action, as the name suggests, is a jigging one. That is to say, the rod tip is raised and lowered, to a distance of about six inches or so, continually. The lure rises and falls in the water (erratically because of its offset eye) and looks positively like nothing at all ever likely to be found in the water anywhere! And yet, the action is tantalising and obviously attractive to fish.

Special jig hooks can be bought, I believe, in this country, but even if they are unavailable it is a simple matter to pinch a shot on to a regular hook with a turned-down eye and make your own.

There are odd times when the magic just isn't there, and they are then ignored completely but, as a rule, there is at least some reaction on the fish's part.

I once showed one to a salmon, with strange results. I could see it lying under the bridge and it remained completely oblivious of all I had to offer. It almost yawned with the boredom of it all until I showed it the jig. Then it woke up and moved. With a great swirl of its tail it made off downstream leaving a great bow wave behind it.

I never saw it again and I still do not know whether I dare take the same chance with the next one I spot. It could prove to be deadly but perhaps it would be better to leave well alone.

In the darkness of a summer night in South Wales I once hooked and lost a large sea trout on a pink-and-white jig after working it through the pool for a steady ten minutes or so. The hooks of these jigs are soft—they are made to straighten when caught in underwater snags—and the power of the sea trout (it *might* have been a salmon), helped by the strong current, was too much for it.

I have had reaction from carp that I could see without being seen, and I believe there are times when all species of fish could well be tempted by correctly presented jigs.

I have lost count of the numbers of fish I have caught in the USA on them, and if I had to be restricted to artificial lures and had to choose one particular type I would plump unhesitatingly for the jig.

In clear water it is deadly for pike. I have used it through ice and watched a pike eye it, utterly fascinated, until it could restrain itself no longer. Then it launched itself at it with unbelievable speed and (as I should have known all along that it would do) took off with it and a yard or so of monofil.

That is one of the snags regarding jigs for pike. They do not work properly on the end of a wire trace, and even a thick, nylon shock leader impairs the action considerably. They more or less have to be worked on regular leaders, or reel lines.

Weight, of course, is a deciding factor. The ones I have used to the most deadly effect have been in the region of $\frac{1}{32}$ ounce. Often, using a fly rod, I have been down to $\frac{1}{96}$ ounce, and occasionally I have increased to $\frac{1}{16}$ ounce. I have many others much heavier, and these will indeed work well on thick nylon or wire leaders, but they do not appear as attractive to pike as those in the lightweight range fished on, say, 5–6-pound leaders.

Fishing for pike with such tackle is, of course, a risky business, but I am sure that if I had taken stock over the years, I would have shown a very high success rate. I do not pretend to understand why but, despite the fierceness of their attack, most pike are only liphooked and usually stay attached. And I am convinced that those that manage to break away are not in the least inconvenienced by the small, single, soft wire hook left behind.

Unhooking a pike to return it to the water is no problem when only single jig hooks are involved. Soft wire singles are so much easier to remove than trebles—even the modern barbless tackles so popular today.

Clear water is essential, in my opinion, for all kinds of artificial-lure pike fishing, but because there is so little to see it is possibly even more so for jig fishing. Big flashing spoons, fiercely vibrating bar spoons and violent-actioned plugs are perhaps in with a chance of being detected in murky water. Deadbaits either left to fish on the bottom or retrieved very, very slowly are likely to be detected by their natural smell, but the little jig needs clear water to be seen. That, I believe, is its only failing, but its convenience and remarkable efficiency make it a lure to be considered seriously by all pike anglers.

Feathered adornments, and hair-wing or buck-tail streamer effects are important additions to the bare jig hook but so too are head colours. It is impossible to lay down any hard-and-fast rules regarding colour combinations, but it is important to be able to ring the changes. A successful combination today will possibly fail miserably tomorrow, and I can recall many times when I have sat over a fish for a long time with no reaction, yet have caught it within seconds of finding the colour for the day. I believe this applies to all kinds of plugs, spoons and spinners too.

One kind of embellishment that may be added to a regular jig is the incredible American plastic worm (which I have mentioned in 'Smell Appeal'). You may be excused for doing so, but please do not laugh. There is so much we do not know.

When you look at a plastic worm smelling of liquorice or aniseed, you may find it hard to believe that this is the hottest lure to have hit the American fishing scene this decade. You cannot imagine any self-respecting fish coming within yards of it, much less taking it with enthusiasm. But they do. More American bass have been taken on plastic worms during the past ten years than on all the other lures put together. It is hard to see why and the temptation, naturally, is to put it down to the fact that American fish behave a lot differently from ours. Our fish would have none of this nonsense: the difference between a juicy fat lobworm and an inert piece of plastic is just too obvious. That is an absolute fact, of course. A length of ruby-coloured plastic, looking very much like a string of jelly-babies, would hardly fool a sophisticated bream, tench or perch if it was left to lie motionless on the bottom. But it is not meant to be fished that way. It is designed to be fished on the move and should in fact be treated like any other spinning lure or plug in this respect.

It is many years since I caught my first pike on a plastic worm in this country. It was a seventeen-pounder and I have never laughed at plastic worms since. I still use them regularly, not to the exclusion of other lures or baits, but certainly with regard to special conditions and situations. They have no advantage over real worms for bottom-feeding fish, but they can undoubtedly be put to good use for pike if mounted on jig hooks. Their main virtue is that they can be rendered almost completely snag-proof because the hook always rides uppermost. That makes all the difference in the world in my book.

It means that you can toss a lure into a veritable jungle of tree roots and sunken branches. It means that stump-lined bays and margins of reed mace can be covered effectively without the loss of bait or lure. And that in turn means that you can come to terms with the pike that lie up in such places and remain virtually impossible to reach with multi-hooked lures or baits.

The method of fishing a big plastic-worm jig is the same as any other. Accurate casts, varied retrieves at all depths and an up-and-down movement of the rod tip to liven up the action are the only real requirements.

They will never take the place of real fish baits, of course, nor will they supersede plugs and spoons, but fished on jig hooks for special situations they can sometimes make a world of difference.

The Boxing Day 'Hunt'

There's something special about Boxing Day piking. It has an appeal which doesn't seem to be present in other forms of fishing and even some of my died-in-the-wool trout-fishing friends indulge in this once-a-year pastime. It is a tradition and it is usually treated light-heartedly. No one is really out for blood on Boxing Day.

Last year we chose to fish the river, largely because there seemed to be a great many pike actively present. We were not interested in catching monsters but, looking forward to some action with smaller and more co-operative fish, we kept on the move. We caught a few, but we kept no records: it wasn't that kind of day—nor should it ever be. Boxing Day piking is an exercise in relaxation and should be played according to your mood.

Watching an anchored deadbait or a tethered livebait can be relaxing as well as productive, and it may well suit the sportsman who has over-indulged the previous day and wants a restful day, but I always feel the need for exercise and choose the more active kind of fishing. Last year we played around with artificials for the greater part of the day and achieved moderate success by moving up and down the two-mile stretch of narrow river.

We had our problems, of course, not the least of which was the amount of weed still present in the river. The pike were in some pretty tricky positions and we lost a number of rather expensive spoons and plugs trying to get at them, all of which made us change over eventually to mounted deadbaits. Losing a deadbait mount comprising a couple of treble hooks and a piece of wire does not come quite as expensive as losing a plug costing £2 or so. And, for that matter, the deadbait (we used sprats from the local fish merchant) is probably more effective anyway.

There are many ways of presenting a mounted sprat, but few anglers bother to try fishing one on a float. Some years ago, a young friend of mine tired of casting and began trotting his sprat down river below a small pike bung. I thought then he was wasting his time, but he wasn't.

Letting his tackle drift on in front of him he guided his bait into the likely lies, holding back here, swinging across the current there, and actually steering the bait where he wanted it. Very little casting was necessary but it was, nevertheless, an extremely mobile form of fishing. And the pike liked it! To be fair, he lost more pike than he landed but the idea obviously worked.

There's nothing new in fishing, of course. Years ago the old exponents of pike fishing in Yorkshire's Horsey Mere used herrings supported by big pike bungs and allowed the wind and waves to impart the movement. This was the same thing on a smaller scale and the flow of the river imparted the movement.

Since then we have improved matters. We have learned that a thin two-inch strip of lead pushed into the body of the dead sprat can be twisted and bent into many different shapes which give the bait added movement and make it appear very attractive to pike in both rivers and still waters.

Pike are reputed to be solitary creatures, lurking in hiding to attack any unsuspecting small fish which happen to cross their path. In some waters, at some times of the year, this is perfectly true, and the angler who regularly fishes a particular water will quickly learn the whereabouts of the pike's lies. Once located they can be relied on to produce fish on more than one occasion throughout the year. Often, when a pike is caught and removed from a particular lie, another fish of similar proportions will eventually take up residence in the same place sometime later. The casual pike angler is unlikely to know these lies, however, and will have to search diligently.

There are waters where pike lies, as such, are practically non-existent. These are uniform, rather characterless stretches of either river, lake, canal or reservoir, where there are very few natural features to encourage a pike to become domiciled. In these circumstances the pike, for some reason best known to themselves, often accumulate in small groups. (I am not here referring to the regular and well-known end-of-season accumulations which take place prior to spawning but to pike which appear to be following the irregular movements of the food fishes.)

This has little to do with casual Christmas-time piking but it helps make the point that the angler who *hunts* his pike will almost certainly do better than the angler who waits for them to come to him.

It would take many years of controlled research to discover just why a group of average-sized pike should be in one spot today and, say, a hundred yards farther along the canal tomorrow, but for practical purposes it is enough to know that it happens. It applies especially to big lakes and reservoirs. Today, for instance, we could take the punt and row it upwind to the far end of the lake and drift back slowly along a certain line picking up a pike here and there. Tomorrow, the same drift could produce nothing, whereas one twenty yards to the left or right could be a winner.

It is *always* worth repeating a successful drift when pike fishing. Just as the reservoir trout angler gets 'on a line' of fish, so can the pike angler cover the same line several times with a good chance of a fish each time.

On big exposed lakes, it is often difficult to drift slowly enough to cover the water efficiently. All too soon the boat or punt is carried downwind and another long haul is necessary before the drift line can be covered again. In these circumstances it is better by far to anchor solidly and fish out an area systematically before drifting downwind again.

The move need not cover more than a few yards. It can be accomplished by lifting the anchor briefly and holding it a few feet off the bottom until the boat has drifted into a new position.

This way, a very big area of water can be covered effectively with a minimum of effort, and all methods, including livebaiting, deadbaiting and spinning, are suited to its application.

With good outdoor clothing to keep the outer man warm and a little something for the inner man as well, there's no better way of spending a Boxing Day than in a light-hearted hunt for pike. And it doesn't matter much whether it succeeds or not.

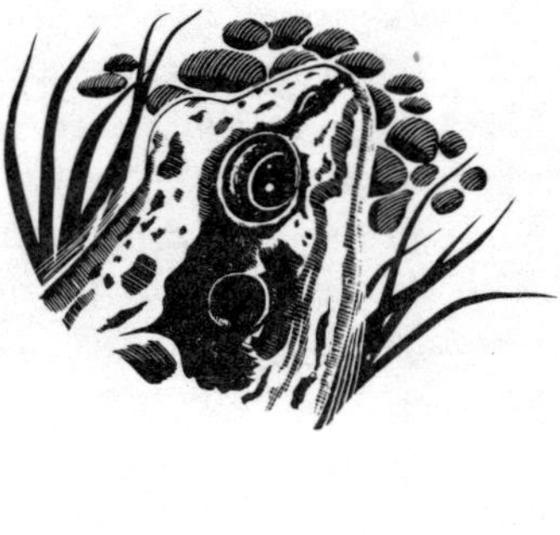

The Wayward Wind

I'll admit that I don't like fishing in a wind, but for a great deal of the time available to me in the winter it is that, or not fishing at all. And as I don't like to go long without wetting a line, there have been periods when I've been blown off the lake more often than I've managed to stay on it. Fishing in a gale is bad enough, but trying to handle a boat at the same time is murder, so when unable to get afloat, I have concentrated a great deal on bank fishing for still-water pike (because floods have fouled up my river fishing so often), and I have been able to pay more attention to rudd and roach at the same time.

When you're controlling a boat, fishing a line of drift, searching out the known hotspots and generally moving around in search of pike, you're busy enough without trying to put up an extra outfit and fish for something else. But you can from the bank, and if you're not too deadly serious about your fishing you can usually watch the pike rod out of the corner of your eye while you fish with a little more concentration for roach and rudd. Or you can do as I sometimes do—attach a sensitive buzzer to the pike outfit. By sensitive, I mean something that will register a bite without the fish feeling too much resistance, but which will, at the same time, not register 'bites' every time the wind catches the line. I find an ordinary carp bite-alarm set a bit more open than usual is good enough provided the line is allowed to tighten briefly when a fish takes. It's only the initial warning I require. Once I'm aware that there's something going on I watch the line for further developments.

If you leave the bale arm of a reel open and set the alarm very delicately in a high wind you're forever getting false warnings, so, although I still leave the bale arm open, I hold the line down on the ground with a piece of stick or push it into a paper-clip taped on to the rod butt. Anything, in fact, that will prevent it from running through the rod rest without any hindrance at all. I *want* the line to tighten against the bite alarm antenna. I *want* it to close the contacts and give me that brief warning before it starts running out. After that I don't care if it bleeps or not. It's not dark and I can see what's going on!

It can be a bit boring sometimes, watching two rods set up for deadbaiting, waiting for one of them to show signs of a bite, and I don't think it does any harm to do a spot of roach fishing while you're waiting. It may be a different story on waters where a super-fast strike is needed the moment a pike picks up the bait, but I've never found that kind of action necessary on the waters I fish.

If I'm concentrating on catching pike and nothing but pike, I prefer to cover fresh water continually and to go after the pike instead of waiting for them to come to me. But for a relaxed kind of fishing, where it isn't the end of the world if you *don't* catch anything, it's pleasant to combine two kinds of fishing. And when I do this I find I'm concentrating more on the roach or rudd than on the pike (which I'm usually better geared to catch).

I like to fish in comfort but I've found over the years that it doesn't pay to sit and fish with the wind. It's better by far to fish into it, despite the difficulties of casting and bite registration. There are all sorts of reasons put forward for it, and I don't suppose any of us know the real answers, but it's generally true that more roach and rudd bites are likely to occur along the bank which is taking the main force of the wind. I've often wondered if it's because surface food is blown in that direction and whether or not it builds up into a concentration that attracts fish. One thing I'm fairly certain about is that it has little or nothing to do with temperature because there's very little variation anywhere on shallow lakes at this time of year.

Whatever the reason, it's a fair bet that if roach and rudd are piled up in one area, it won't be too long before pike show there too, and I'm very much convinced that the act of catching roach helps start pike feeding too. It's been proved enough times, at least to convince *me*.

Punching a light float tackle out into the teeth of a high wind is not easy and it's difficult to be accurate. But a situation often arises when the wind is so strong that an undercurrent develops which will actually tow a float tackle *away* from the bank, despite the fact that the wind is blowing *towards* it. It's very much the same sort of thing that develops in a turbulent weir pool. If you know just where to drop the tackle the undertow will pull it in under the weir sill. So, quite often, it's not necessary to cast at all, but instead to drop the float tackle in a yard or two out and let it chug away to where you want it!

I've heard it said that shallow lakes aren't really worth fishing in winter (except for pike) but I'm convinced that many of them would produce other fish if they were exploited more. I fished down at the Warrells Lake at Wotton recently and although we lost a lot of roach and rudd two years ago, the water is stiff with them again. Most of those I caught were small, but there were some nice half-pounders among them which pleased me. They fed about a foot off the bottom, which isn't at all unusual for the water in question, and there didn't appear to be any real hotspots. The bites came from almost anywhere as long as the depth setting was right.

Another day it might have been different, of course. The bites might have come when the bait was dragging bottom or an inch or so above it. There's usually a pattern, but in these conditions it doesn't seem to be one of pinpoint accuracy with regard to distance.

Peter Drennan had recently made me up some beautiful floats which have thin peacock-quill antennas and carry a little more than two swanshots. They were ideal for this situation and would undoubtedly cope with almost any tricky wind problem. I shotted them down as Peter had told me, and attached them loosely through the end ring with a small shot pinched either side. In other words I had one shot pinched above the float and another just below it—plus the bulk and other shots distributed below that. Despite their considerable carrying capacity these floats registered bites from small fish remarkably well in a howling wind. I found out, too, that it was necessary (as Peter had already told me) to pinch those two holding shots on about two inches apart so that the float would 'fold' when I struck.

Stillwater roach and rudd tend to get well mixed up on some waters at this time of year and ours are no exception. They behave in much the same manner and feed at much the same depths.

I started out using maggots, but I caught better (though fewer) fish on crust—which, in any event, is a favourite bait with me for a great part of the season. I found I had to pinch a tiny shot on the hook shank, however, to overcome the crust's buoyancy.

Strangely, I didn't get a pike at all (though I missed one run) but who wants pike when the roach are 'on'?

These very windy conditions do not necessarily please me but they *do* intrigue me, and for a good many years brother Ken and I have always headed for the windward side of the lake whether we've been after either pike baits or quality roach.

I suppose it's the memory of many previous catches that draws us. We can't forget some of the great bags we've had in years gone by when we were much more serious and results meant so much more to us than they do now. If there was a choice, of course, I guess both of us would prefer no wind at all, but when it's there I know we both like to look it straight in the face.

No Problem!

'What will you do,' said one of my friends, 'if you catch a twenty-nine-pounder this week?'

We were on the plane for Dublin, heading, eventually, for the River Erne in County Cavan where we were to spend a week pike fishing. He knew, of course, that I had a pike just under that weight mounted in a glass case above my desk, and being aware of the cost of taxidermy he wondered if I would go to the same expense and trouble again for a fish slightly bigger.

To be honest the thought had never occurred to me. As far as I was concerned a $28\frac{1}{4}$-pounder was my top weight. I couldn't hope for a bigger fish and I said so. 'But,' I said, 'if by chance I do happen to get one, I shall be faced with a real problem.'

After all, who could sit and look at a mounted twenty-eight-pounder knowing that he had caught a bigger one? Naturally a bigger one would have to be mounted too. On the other hand, how do you convince your wife and others, to whom you have said many times that you don't like stuffed fish anyway, that you've got to go in for yet another piece of taxidermy?

Well, the problem wouldn't arise, I was sure, and so I put the matter from my mind. All week long, however, my friends (if such they be) kept reminding me of the ever-present possibility and of the problems I would face if a bigger pike came my way.

It was all great fun, but on the Thursday the joke misfired. A big pike took hold of my tiny dead roach bait as I bumped it across the fast current of the River Erne.

It pulled away slowly and doggedly. I could make no impression on it with my 10-pound line and my three friends began to offer advice and estimate its weight. Twelve pounds they said, maybe more. Later they said it could be twenty or even twenty-five pounds. I had been playing it for ten minutes at that stage and it seemed then that I was the calmest person present.

The fish suddenly stripped off about forty yards of line, headed for the shallow bank near the island and leapt clear of the water. Then we *knew* it was a big one.

It took me twenty minutes in all to beat it and finally it was bundled up the bank and on to the official scales. It weighed just over thirty-two pounds and I was no longer calm!

Problems? There were none at all. Well, none except for those involved in getting it back to the hotel, packing it in a wooden coffin, getting the airline to accept it as excess baggage, persuading the Customs officer that it really *was* a dead fish and rushing it across London to the taxidermist!

Those problems are over now, and even my wife has learned to accept the second glassy-eyed monster that graces the wall of my study.

Salmon and 'Soppies'

When you travel up to a famous salmon river like the Tweed, full of hope and enthusiasm, and fail to get so much as a touch, it's a bit disappointing. When you travel up with a dyed-in-the-wool seafisher, who prefers beachcasters to spinning rods, shark harnesses to waders and 26-ounce pirks to Devon minnows, and *he* catches a salmon, it's embarrassing. But when you have to suffer talk about how easy salmon are to catch by someone who 'obviously must be superior in angling skill' and who thinks he'll 'write some articles or perhaps a book about it', etc., etc., for the next two days, it's soul destroying!

I mean, there was this great big fellow, tall as a church, wide as an office block, and supposedly gentle as a lamb, throwing out Devons and cranking them in with a bored look on his face and a no-hope look in his eyes. I could tell he was having great difficulty in *not* casting 150 yards each throw, and I knew he was just wishing that the Tweed might have been twice as wide as it was. That would have made it more interesting for him, I'm sure, even if he'd never so much as seen a fish. But he lost the bored expression when he hooked a salmon and began hopping about on one foot calling for help! Only when it was safely on the bank did he revert to his original nonchalance and begin to inform us that 'there's nothing to it, really'.

Makes you sick!

Of course I'm really delighted that Les Moncrieff caught one. He has now, as I write this, been twice and has caught one each time, but I still think that that's no reason for him to keep informing me that he *always* catches a salmon *every* time he goes salmon fishing. On the other hand I wish I could say the same thing.

It's a tricky game as far as I'm concerned and because I do not seem to be able to apply any logic to the business of *why* salmon behave the way they do, I soon tire of fishing for them. I'm absolutely certain that if there was not a great deal of pleasure to be derived from fishing a certain style well, and from using good tackle with skill, there would be fewer salmon fishers around. The truth is that, generally speaking, you have to make a great many casts before you're likely to catch a salmon and if you don't actually enjoy the mechanics of casting and 'fishing' the bait, lure or fly, you're not likely to go into raptures about salmon fishing. The only real thrill comes with the fish on the end.

I can readily understand the pleasures a good salmon fly fisher can feel when he works down a pool methodically and with precision, covering the water well and enjoying the sight and feel of a good cast well executed time and time again.

I know that I can enjoy flicking a pike spoon to a difficult lie, figuring out where a pike might be, working the spoon continually and making it behave the way I want it to at the depth I choose. I can do that with pike tackle in still water, but I can't really come to terms with it on a deep, fast-flowing river when there is nothing to indicate where a salmon is likely to be. It's all very fine for a gillie or boatman to tell me that such and such is a good taking spot, or that I'll be covering taking water in my next two or three casts, but I like to figure things out for myself and to know *why*. Perhaps, if I fished the same water for salmon for a number of years, I'd come to terms with the how, where and when of it all. But I doubt if I'd ever know the whys.

That's why I found myself wondering and asking about the roach of the Tweed once more. I caught them years ago and I know that there was no problem then about getting permission to fish for them. Was it the same now? I asked.

I was told that there were still plenty of good roach to be caught there, and that certain waters were open to coarse fishing on payment of, I believe, thirty pence per day. But I was also told that these permits to fish were becoming increasingly difficult to obtain and that waters where they were once issued are now becoming fewer each season. The reason? It seems that some coarse fishers will never learn that payment of thirty pence does not give anyone the right to obstruct salmon anglers who may have to pay twice that number of *pounds* for a day's fishing.

I was told stories of salmon pools being monopolised by coarse fishers who had parked themselves under umbrellas and refused to move when asked. I heard of coarse fishers' cars being parked on the lots set aside for and clearly marked as salmon anglers' car parks and of refusals to move them until the police were sent for. And I was told of the almost impossible task the river keepers and bailiffs had in trying to enforce the no-maggot ruling. It's there on the tickets seemingly, but lots of coarse fishers seem to think it applies to other people—not to them.

I find these facts hard to swallow, but I believe them to be true, and it's my opinion that there will be less and less roach fishing available on the Tweed as the years pass unless it is readily understood that the price paid for permits is chicken feed compared to that paid by salmon anglers. As coarse fishers, we must realise that we have no rights as such. We must, whether we agree or not, accept the fact that the maggot ban has been imposed in order to protect the salmon parr and future salmon returns. Disease and netting have already taken their toll of adult salmon and if the hooking (and often inevitable killing) of salmon parr on maggots is regarded as another threat, we should be wise enough to accept it, and be thankful we can still fish at all.

I was not able to fish for roach, but I enjoyed trying to pick out known roach swims and there was a certain satisfaction in learning that I was right most times. I hope I can go and fish for them when the season opens again.

Meanwhile there's a great deal to be said for a few 'soppies'. Rainbows, I mean—easy ones. There would be no real satisfaction for me in catching a sackful of easy-to-hook fish every time I went out, but just once in a while it's nice to have a few fish hang on and fight like the very devil at the beginning of the trout season.

So, after a blank in Scotland, it was fun to roll up at Little Tring, which had just opened as a trout fishery, and get tied into some small but scrappy little fish.

It was even better next day to limit out on Damerham with trout up to $3\frac{1}{4}$ pounds. I've caught bigger fish many times, and I've had a fair few over twice that weight, but I don't believe I ever had a trout fight as hard or as long as my best one that day. It had been a long time since my arm ached from the landing of one fish, but that's how it was. In fact, if all Damerham fish fight like those I caught I'm glad I didn't get a six-pounder. I'd never have seen it on the tackle I was using!

It's true they were 'soppies', as far as hooking them went, but there was nothing soppy about them from then on. And they did my morale a power of good.

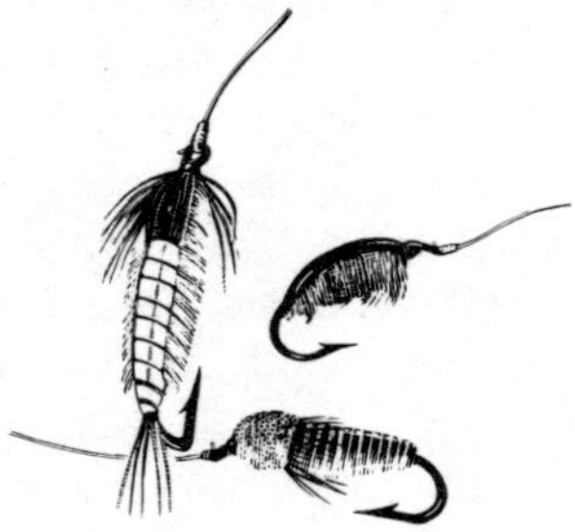

Suspense With Worms

I'm not too sure whether I'm pleased or not about what's in Arthur Oglesby's book *Salmon*. Well, what I mean is that he refers to me in it as an expert at worming for salmon—which could, perhaps, be regarded as a back-handed compliment!

And knowing that Arthur doesn't really care for worming (in fact I believe he'd try anything and everything before he finally condescended to handle the messy things), I'm beginning to wonder if it really means anything to be called an expert wormer. Somehow it sounds like being called a poacher! In fact, that's what the late Captain Tommy Edwards *did* call me. I caught quite a few salmon before his very eyes on the worm once and from then on the name stuck.

Never will I forget the time when I was sitting by myself in the lounge of a huge hotel in Scarborough, quietly sipping a drink. It was a quiet room, people were for some reason or other talking in whispers, and I felt rather ill at ease. I knew no one there.

Presently the door opened and in walked Captain Tommy. He spotted me in a second and to my complete embarrassment yelled across the room, 'Hello, you blankety-blank old poacher, what the hell are you doing here?' And to the charming lady who was with him he bellowed, 'This is the fellow I was telling you about. The fellow who catches salmon with WORMS.'

I tried to make believe I didn't hear, that I didn't know this strange fellow, but it was of no use. I felt guilty and wanted to crawl away somewhere quickly.

On reflection, however, I realise that I was being stupid. Tommy had said it all in fun and without wishing to suggest that there was anything wrong in catching salmon on worms. The truth is, of course, that there are occasions when a bunch of worms offers about the only real chance of a fish at all and, where it is legally permitted, there is certainly nothing wrong in using one. It is allowed on most Scottish and northern rivers, but is strictly taboo on some southern rivers. That is rather strange because, in my experience, the worm can only be fished really well in the rocky rivers of the north. The deep and weedy salmon rivers of the south are not really suited to worm fishing, and I feel that it is stupid to ban a method that isn't likely to be very good anyway.

Of course you *can* catch salmon on the worm in southern rivers, but you cannot often do it with any real artistry.

All you can do there is leger with a worm, or a bunch of worms in a pool and wait for a salmon to make the next move. If you can spot a salmon lying deep in a clear pool you can sometimes anchor the worm a few inches from its nose and await results. On occasions the fish will lie and glare at the worm for hours without moving, and then slowly back away and depart. Another time it might move slowly over to it and take it. There's no telling how a salmon will react and you cannot apply any logic to its behaviour.

That kind of worming, however, is very much a hit-or-miss affair just as it would be if practised on a northern river. Not only that, of course: it is an unfair method when other people want to fish too. Hogging a pool with a legered worm and a rod in a forked stick could hardly be regarded as fair angling in those circumstances. Nor could it be considered very skilful.

There is a great deal of difference between that method and the ones I practice. I believe that anyone who has had experience with touch legering can become adept at worming for salmon in the right conditions. Those conditions are usually of low water and stale fish which have seen and refused everything else thrown at them.

Then, if you can fish so that the worms bump along the bottom nicely without becoming snagged and without being whisked away in the current, you are presenting the bait correctly. Inevitably, the first attempt is either too light or too heavy and the casting weight has to be adjusted to suit the current, which is not at all easy in fast and rocky water, but is essential to good fishing.

A simple swanshot link is probably the most versatile leger to use. It is easy to add a shot to, or remove a shot from, the separate link until the right weight is found. Then, with finger lightly on the line, you can feel the weight bumping down and across the current. And you can feel the first gentle and steady pull on the line when the salmon takes an interest for the first time. You may have to make a hundred casts before this happens because this method is just as active as spinning or fly fishing—with the added chore of replenishing the worms every so often. When you *do* feel something happening—do nothing. Just leave the line slack (bale arm open on a fixed-spool reel) and let the fish take. It will try to swallow the worm (which is strange because salmon do not really feed in fresh water, as we all know) but it is doubtful if it will be able to do so. Then it will move back to its original lie and, barring accident, will be yours.

The more you practise it, the easier it becomes and the more you begin to understand the business of casting and fishing *exactly* as if you were spinning deep and slow. Sooner or later the bait has to be presented to a salmon and with any luck at all you'll feel the gentle, *slow* pull as it takes. All very exciting, but not half as exciting as worming in the crystalline waters of small northern spate rivers.

Few salmon run up them, and those that do are extraordinarily difficult to catch. In times of spate they may fall to the legered worm. On a rising flood they can (if you are expert enough, which I am not) be caught on a fly, and, on a falling water, they will occasionally take a spinner. For the greater part of the time, however, they will accept nothing. There they lie, each one in its own little haven of unbelievably clear water, scared of the slightest shadow and decidedly touchy.

But, if you can by sheer bloody-minded persistence present a couple of worms on fairly fine tackle before a salmon's nose, tease it, tempt it, harass it and give it no peace, *without so much as showing a hint of yourself or your rod*, you just might after a long, long time, hook it.

No one understands it, really, and perhaps it's just as well! You can watch from a vantage point, and see all kinds of antics on the salmon's part. It will back off and approach, nose the worm, lie on top of it, take the very tip of the tail between its lips and hold it for ten minutes, spit it out and glare at it, swim round the pool with it half in, half out of its mouth, and after all that decide that it is no longer interested. You meanwhile are holding your breath and sweating and trembling and cursing and praying. There never was such a fishing!

And then, suddenly, when you've given up hope, it all happens. The worms that were balanced on the salmon's nose have suddenly disappeared and you realise that they're in its mouth. The salmon is actually attached to the other end of your tackle and you're about to have fun. But the suspense of the fight will never equal the suspense you experienced while it was making up it's mind. That can make an old man of you!

Never on Sundays

Putting four frantic fishermen on to an island that seems to have more water than land, and confining them to four walls for twenty-four hours without allowing them to fish must be like putting a pile of sweets in front of a child and telling it not to touch.

That's just about how it feels to us at present, for on Sunday no fishing is allowed on the Isle of Lewis. Just down the road from us lies a long, narrow loch full of brown trout, not big ones but lovely little pink-fleshed fish which are delicious to eat. We caught some yesterday, but not today.

From the window we can see a great expanse of blue ocean with a beach of silver sand, and big rock islands covered with seaweed and clams, breaking up its vastness into a hundred different bays. They tell us here that mackerel sometimes come into the bays and that there are haddock to be caught from the small rowing boat. But not on the Sabbath!

A few miles away, the Red River runs from Loch Raonasgail to the sea at Carnish Bay. Salmon and sea trout run up its full length and are already in the loch. Others accumulate with each tide at the road-bridge pool when there is sufficient water in the river itself. Today the river is low, but it is raining hard and tomorrow we might just be in business. But not today!

Today we drink tea, while we prepare tackle that needs no preparing and generally while away the water hours.

In the evening, Malcolm the keeper calls and shows us the way to the big loch. It's a four-mile walk across rough country and we are not too sure whether we want to struggle that far with all our gear. Perhaps we can lighten the load when, and if, we decide to go.

We've looked at a dozen more trout lochs and we've been shown a place where we might even catch sea trout in the salt water. Malcolm has given us some special salt-water lures for the job. Now all we can do is wait for tomorrow.

Monday morning came at last. It was a hard pull across the moor to the small but beautiful loch that holds the 'wee pink troot'.

Bob MacDonald, an American friend, took his ultra-light spinning rod, Ken and I took bait rods and Arthur took his fly rod. We really didn't care too much what we used, but we wanted to find out the best method for the water. Above all, we needed trout to eat. There are no shops here and we had only basic hard rations until the meal van called.

It didn't take us too long to find out that Ken and I were wasting our time with worms and maggots despite the fact that I doubt very much if the trout here ever saw any of the latter.

Arthur failed pretty miserably too with his fly rod and only managed to catch two small fish. Bob, on the other hand, did just what he said he'd do: catch enough fish for all of us to eat. We could hear the swish of his little ultra-light rod on the other side of the loch and every so often we'd look up and watch him reel in a trout that leapt and splashed all the way to the net.

We ate all twelve of them for lunch and it was pretty galling to have to keep listening to the constant reminders that the meal was provided by R. MacDonald of the USA!

The tide was in at the bridge pool when we arrived there in the evening, and Ken was at the water's edge before I had my tackle assembled. I watched him make his first cast, saw him draw in the line by hand and make contact with the big, free-lined worm before letting it fish through the pool, and forgot everything but the landing net when I saw him bend into his first fish. A sea trout of about a pound.

I tried to tie a hook but my fingers were trembling with excitement and I fumbled badly. Time was short. This tide would last but a brief hour and I wanted to make the most of it, but I dropped the hook along with the rod when Ken hit another fish about the same size. Two casts, two sea trout. On the other bank, Arthur was casting his fly; further down Bob was spinning, but the action was all around Ken and me.

Finally, I made it and let the worm swing round into the deep pool halfway across the river. I had my chances but I was too anxious, too excited, too determined to catch up with Ken, and I made a mess of things.

I missed two good takes and then felt a big fish (I *know* it was a big fish) pick up the bait and swim powerfully upstream. I thought I'd timed it right but obviously I hadn't. My strike brought back a thin band of worm and an otherwise bare hook, and I swore in disgust.

A great silver shape leapt clear of the water in front of me and landed back with an almighty splosh. I was about to remark to Ken about it when I saw that he was attached to it. Of course, I panicked. I always panic when *someone else* is tied on to a good fish!

Ken kept calm, told me not to worry, told us he knew what to do, told me he wasn't going to 'horse' it, told me he'd tell me when he was ready for the net. And the fish, spending more time out of the water than in it, made great surging rushes up towards the arches of the bridge, while I stood by helplessly with the net ready in the shallow water.

The issue was never really in doubt, however, and in spite of my anxiety Ken slid the fish over the net and I lifted it out, realising at the same time that the tide had risen so much that we were now stranded on the shingle beach several yards from the shore.

But it didn't matter any more—so we'd get wet feet, so maybe we'd have to wade ashore. Little we cared that the tackle bags were floating away on the tide. These were the fish we'd come for—the most exciting fish and often the most difficult fish we'd ever encountered.

We caught several more smaller fish and two more weighing about a pound each before the tide ebbed and we found ourselves on dry land and moved, but Ken's fish, a $5\frac{1}{2}$-pounder, was the highlight of the day.

We took them back to the cottage in triumph and had a 'wee dram' with Malcolm to celebrate our first real catch.

'I'm delighted for ye,' he said, 'A salmon on your verra first day!'

We didn't argue with him. If he wanted it to be a salmon, so be it. But it wasn't—it was a sea trout just like all the others. And when we catch our first salmon we'll be able to prove it!

A Touch of Sea Trout

Personal business took me up to Lancashire and I thought it a bit silly to go thus far without stretching my journey to include an hour or two with the sea trout.

It was the tail end of the season, and I didn't expect to do anything spectacular, but I'm very fond of sea trout and the problems they present. And I'm also very fond of applying coarse-fish tactics for them on a water that is not restricted as to method. So I made arrangements.

'We need water badly,' said my host, Hugh, 'but you could be in luck. At any rate there are fish in some of the pools if you're smart enough to catch them.'

Two days before I was due to set off, it rained, and rained, and rained. Our local rivers and all waters south of us were swollen and bank high. I travelled north full of hope—and into glorious sunshine! When I arrived, the little northern river had not had the benefit of a single raindrop. The fish were there, grey and still in the clear, deep water, anxious to move up, scared by the slightest shadow and not, I thought, in taking mood.

They reminded me of summers past when I had spent short, warm nights fishing fly (badly) and worm (effectively) in the darkness, and I determined to spend some of my allotted sleeping time in this pursuit. But I was not nearly as confident as I had been in previous summers.

I decided to go and spot during daylight so that I could be sure of my line of cast after dark, and I was on my way to do just that when Hugh suggested that I might care to try to fish in daylight. I was dubious, however, knowing very well how easy it is to scare these fish. The movement of a leafy branch above their heads, a shadow thrown on the water, the 'plip' of a single split shot or the entry of a free-lined lobworm, the flash of a fishing rod or the sight of a bald head peering through the long grass have all scared them in the past.

I know it from experience. And I know too, or at least I am satisfied that it is so, that fish scared by day are less likely to take after dark. But it *was* a long time until dark and, after all, I *did* only have a few hours to spare.... So I sneaked down to the meadow dub, and hid in the shade of the tall oak tree.

Under the far bank I could see the shapes of, perhaps, fifty fish of all sizes, and because of the extreme clarity of the water I put up a light touch-leger rod, and 3-pound line.

I had worms, maggots and a supply of sea trout flies and lures of all kinds which I hoped to use in another pool after dark. But, for the time being, I thought it better to fish at long range with fine tackle and disturb the fish as little as possible. I opted for two maggots on a No. 14 hook with a 2-pound link, and a single swanshot leger fixed three feet from the bait.

Knowing how little these fish moved around during the day unless they *were* scared, I realised that I had to put the bait right in among them. I did this by casting well past them and winding back slowly until I judged it to be in the right place.

A flash of silver on the bottom suggested that my tackle had disturbed an odd fish, but it also indicated that the bait was where I wanted it. I crouched behind the tree, holding the line on the tip of my finger, prepared to wait for a long time for the first bite, and was amazed and taken completely unawares by a sudden snatch on the rod tip.

I reacted quite automatically and struck into a fish. A sea trout of two to three pounds leaped clear of the water and headed upstream. I couldn't believe my luck. A fish within seconds and it was already headed away from the others! My luck was short-lived, however—the fish leaped again and threw the small hook.

And that, I thought, is that. Such thing's don't happen twice in one session. And up to a point I was right. I didn't get another similar snatch, and I didn't hook another two-to-three-pound sea trout. But I *did* get nine more bites which resulted in eight fish.

They were delicate bites that needed a little concentration and a fast reaction, but the little rod dotted them all but one. These fish were, indeed, a lot smaller: there wasn't a pounder among them, but they were all of takeable size. I could, I'm sure, have taken a lot more had I so wished, but in little more than an hour I felt I'd caught enough for the time being, and I moved upstream to sit over a very much bigger fish I'd spotted earlier.

I couldn't tell, because of the strange light, whether it was a sea trout or a salmon, but I suspect it was the latter. I dropped a big worm into the clear pool and sat very, very still. A dozen or more times the fish cruised over it and either ignored it completely or failed to notice it was there. I don't know which is more nerve-racking—that, or fishing floating crust for carp!

I'd like to say I nailed it eventually but I didn't. I twitched the worm once and held my breath while the fish ambled over to take a look before deciding that it wasn't interested. So I gave it best.

Going back to the meadow dub I studied the shoal of smaller fish once more, and suddenly I noticed they were twisting and flashing in the current and occasionally flopping along the bottom sideways on. Past experience told me that this behaviour often indicates a change in conditions, that rain could be on the way, and that I ought to make the most of the remaining daylight hours. But in that brief interval, the whole pattern had changed. There were no more bites, the fish were now very restless and could no longer be tempted to take. It was as if they had sensed the imminent rain and were preparing to move on the moment the level rose sufficiently for them to do so.

I had had the best of it, and it was indeed fortunate that I had been at the water's edge for that brief taking period. Now it was over, and as I headed for home the rain began to fall heavily. In twelve hours or so, with luck, the river would be in full spate and some fortunate angler in the right place at the right time would probably get the big fish I had tried for.

For several days the sea trout, those that remained, would somehow be stimulated into taking again and someone would have one of those memorable nights that we hear about but seldom experience ourselves.

I had to leave a golden opportunity but I have to admit that I don't often travel six hundred miles, catch eight sea trout (albeit small) and arrive back home again within twenty-four hours!

Some would say it wasn't worth it, but then they've never known the joys and frustrations of the little spate river.

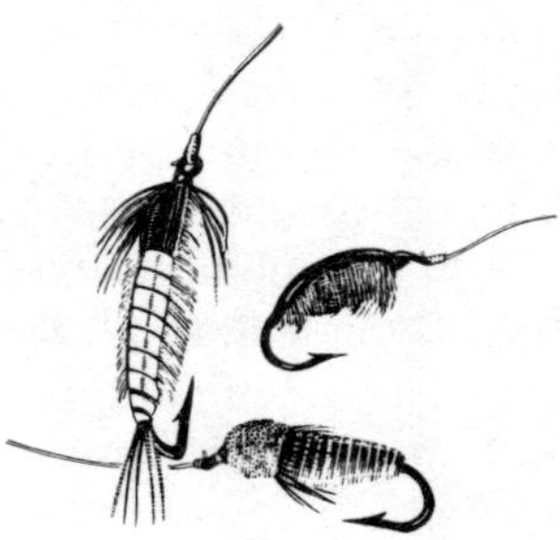

'Dibbling' for Grayling

One September a group of us were standing on a bridge, gazing into the water as all anglers are inclined to do, and someone said: 'There's a small salmon.' The dark shape dropped back out of sight, then moved out into the current again in full view.

The behaviour was salmon-like, but that fish was no salmon. It was an enormous grayling—quite the biggest I have ever seen—and I marked it for later in the year. It's never shown again since, of course. Grayling are like that.

We might have tried for it at the time, but somehow grayling are not looked upon as summer or autumn fish. They're winter fish and can usually be relied upon to feed at some time or other on the coldest of days. So we left it until the time was ripe and tried later in the year: I'd better say at once, however, that we didn't catch it!

The current where we had first spotted it was now a lot stronger and the lie was almost unfishable, so we fished instead in a deeper pool just above.

The grayling we caught were not big by any means, but along with some quality dace, they helped swell the overall bag, and made for good sport and, later, good eating. But we lost a number of fish during the day because we were obliged to use hooks too small for the task.

The river was crystal clear, the fish were very cautious, and we felt all along that we were handicapped, but could see no real answer to the problem.

Maggots and casters, fished singly on No. 16 hooks, produced bites. Anything bigger produced nothing, and on the rare occasions when a bigger grayling took hold, it would back out into the current which it used to help it escape. Small hooks pull clear easily when grayling have to be bullied upstream, and, as they're soft-mouthed generally, these bigger fish almost invariably come adrift.

Traditionally it's always the bigger fish that get away but on this occasion it happened to be true. In heavy water I can see no real answer to this problem while the fish remain choosy about bait and hook size. All you can do is carry on and hope that some of the fish stay hooked—which they do.

But there is a dodge that's always worth trying in these circumstances and I tried it successfully towards the end of the day. I picked out a gaudy yellow nondescript fly, weighted it with a swanshot and 'dibbled' where I'd been getting most bites.

Please don't ask me why grayling should be fussy about bait size but still be prepared to take a chunk of yellow wool, fur, hair, feather or what-have-you, because I do not know. All I know is that sometimes they will, and on this occasion I winkled out three better fish from under the rod tip.

The lure is simply a variation of the old 'grasshopper', a lead-bound, wool-dressed hook often used effectively in Yorkshire streams. It doesn't have to be too precise—the importance lies in getting it down to the fish and making it work.

Downstream of me I saw another angler lose a fish. 'It was huge,' he said as he baited up again with trembling fingers. 'Came off right at the net.' I have a feeling it was the fish we'd seen from the bridge earlier in the year, and if that is the case it will have learned yet another lesson in the art of survival.

Stret-Pegging

'Stret-pegging,' said a tackle-dealer friend some time ago, 'is just a word you fellows made up. I don't even know where it comes from or what it means.'

Funny that. I don't know where it comes from either, but I do know what it means and I'm sure none of my friends made it up.

Had this been the case I would be a very old man indeed! Stret-pegging, or stretting as it is sometimes called, goes back to the days when anglers used wooden centre-pin reels and practised what was then known as the 'Nottingham style' for roach, which would be better known today as trotting.

A variation to the Nottingham style was developed to fish a slow-moving, near-bank swim, and it was called, for some unknown reason, 'stret-pegging'. The float was slid up the line so that the tackle was set a foot deeper than the water, the shots were concentrated nearer the hook end but the last eighteen inches or so were left completely free of weights.

After trotting four or five yards the float would be held stationary so that the tackle would rise and fall attractively just off the bottom. The old Thames roach-pole experts used much the same idea without a reel. They referred to it sometimes as 'tight-corking' or 'hanging on'. There were subtle differences, of course, but both methods covered the near-bank area effectively and, by altering the range and angle of the rod, a long swim could be thoroughly exploited.

The rod would, for much of the time, be left in a rest, and when a bite came the float was pulled under very sharply with the result that some fish were missed. Stretting is still used today and in some situations it is still deadly. A rest is used, but only as a support. The rod handle is held all the time, and after stretting in one place for a short time, another yard or so of line is paid out to allow the tackle to search the area immediately downstream. The process is repeated until the whole swim has been covered, or until a particular hotspot has been located.

Just before the end of the season I saw the method used for, of all things, salmon, and I have to admit that I was impressed (as well as water-licked). My friend, who had obviously discovered the whereabouts of the fish in advance, stole my best, very-hard-come-by lobworms and proceeded to floatfish with them.

Stret-pegging for salmon? I'd never heard of it or even considered it, but with a long, coarse-fishing rod he systematically searched the fifty yards of straight near-bank water and caught three fine fish in under two hours.

I didn't complain about the lobworms after that, especially as I was presented with the best of the trio!

And just recently I became aware of the deadliness of the method once again. A shoal of grayling in deep, fast water would not respond to my repeated trotting tactics even though I could see them feeding in the clear pool. So I stret-pegged with my shots concentrated close to the hook and virtually let the tackle fish for itself.

I had eight bites—all of which nearly pulled the rod in and I caught eight fine grayling averaging near a pound each, which is as good an average as you can hope for with any method—old or new.

Tale of a Sail

I'm not much of a sea angler, my experience is very limited, but I do enjoy fishing in estuaries and off the rocks for whatever comes along. I like, too, to catch bass and mullet, particularly mullet, so my ears cocked up when I was told of a spot off the north-west coast where both species could be found close together.

I was sea trout fishing at the time and I fancied having a go at those bass and mullet during the daytime, which is the off-peak time for sea trout. But first I had to locate them and that wasn't easy. I asked around but no one was telling! (Before going any further let me say here and now that I never did find them, so if you want to read about a catch of bass and mullet read no more. The events which led up to my *not* locating them however, were—in retrospect—somewhat hilarious.)

Frank, from the cottage below, came up to the caravan one morning when Ken and I were cooking some herling for breakfast.

'The skipper's getting the boat ready,' he said. 'Care to come for a sail?'

A sail? Now that's something I'd never done and frankly never wanted to do, but when Frank said that we'd be sailing up to the bass and mullet spot I agreed to join them. So did Ken. So did the skipper's big black labrador. And if you think there's room in a small sailing dinghy for four men and a big black labrador, you're mistaken. Well, no—there *is* room if two of you care to sit in the well of the boat and get wet behinds. Not that that made much difference—Ken and I were wet before the boat was launched.

'You'll need gumboots,' announced Frank. 'We'll have to paddle out to launch her.' Ken and I had thigh waders and even they weren't enough to keep the sea out.

We stood—holding that pitching, bucking boat, in what seemed to me to be a gale, but which we were told was a nice breeze—while the skipper messed around, pulling ropes and things, like all sailors do. Every so often a wave would fill our waders. Cold, wet waves, they were; I was miserable before I started. I was even more so when I was told to join the labrador in the big puddle on the bottom of the boat.

I gripped the sides. My fingers trailed in the water and I saw we'd got about three inches of boat clear of the water. Freeboard, do they call it?

'Plenty,' said the skipper. 'Plenty as long as everyone keeps still.' Keeps still? I was too petrified to consider moving, and when the wind filled the sails and we began to pull out towards the open sea I became even more apprehensive.

My seat got wetter and wetter. The big lab decided that this was the life, but that he really should be with his master on the helm. He huff-huffed in my ear and clambered over me with wet and muddy paws.

'Back,' commanded Skipper—and the lab clambered back.

'Where's the bass spot?' I asked.

'Ah, the bass,' said Skipper. 'Yes. I shall go about on the other tack.'

Well, that's what I thought he said, but at that moment a great piece of wood whistled over my head and nearly brained me so I'm not too sure. It only scraped me, though. It didn't actually hit me.

Ken said: 'I've got a wet backside.'

I said: 'I'll be glad when I've had enough of this.'

Skipper said: 'A beautiful piece of seamanship, that.'

And Frank said: 'Rowlocks.'

At that moment the mast snapped clean in two, and with a thunderous noise the whole great mass of canvas and lumps of wood came crashing down to the deck. Luckily most of it landed in the water, but there was a distinct note of urgency in the skipper's voice as he told us what to do to unravel the unholy mess.

'Release the toggle arm on the spiralling sprocket!' he bellowed. Or something like that.

'Cut the blasted rope would be better,' said Frank.

'I've got a wet backside,' said Ken.

And the dog said, 'Oh boy! Master has really excelled himself today. What an exciting day he has arranged for me!' And his wet tail beat a tattoo on my ear.

I did think of going overboard and swimming the two miles to shore, but then I realised I was pinned down like a galley slave and that attempted escape might sink the boat anyway. So I stayed very, very still. Eventually, with it all sorted out, Ken on one oar, Frank on the other, we pulled for shore against a headwind and an ebbing tide.

'Ease up, bow oar. Give way, stroke,' roared Skipper. 'In out, in out.'

It took perhaps an hour of all-out effort by those two very, very good oarsmen to get us back to safety. Skipper was quite exhausted by all his yelling when we finally made it!

Funny now, of course, but in truth, quite serious at the time.

Well, when I've looked at those sailing boats on the big reservoirs I've always thought that the people in them with their funny little sailor's hats and their nautical jargon were a bit strange. Now I know they're completely mad.

After that I was glad to get back to something a little more comfortable. A clean up and a change of clothing and I was soon back to the sea trout fishing.

And it rained all night long and I got wet through.

Nocturnal Happenings

Strange things have happened to me out in the country and at the water's edge. I cannot explain them—there is no explanation.

I cannot, for instance, tell why I am not only uneasy but plain scared stiff to spend the night alone on certain waters, whereas a night spent on the little Cumberland Esk almost demands complete solitude. I have never felt the slightest hint of apprehension there, always preferring to be alone and finding that dawn has always comes too soon.

A night spent alone at either of the lakes at Wotton would, on the other hand, take away my sanity, I'm sure. It was always so. When I fished there night after night, year after year, with two good friends, it was noticeable that we set out our pitches *very* close to each other.

We had a big pontoon there which we had made into a kind of houseboat, and during the close season of 1953 we took it out of the water for repair. Because of the amount of work involved we decided to sleep overnight in the small thatched wooden building on the edge of the lake.

We talked for a long time in the darkness and when we finally drifted into sleep, the whole structure shook as if some large object had struck its side wall. I *know* there was no other human being within miles and it was *not* a practical joke. The thatched roof overhung the structure by six feet all round. It could *not* have been a falling branch.

With strong torches, we ventured out and searched the area but there was nothing to indicate a missile of any kind. To this day we do not know what caused that bang, but years later, when a mutual friend mentioned to the old retired keeper that we were in the habit of sleeping on our boat there, he uttered this warning: 'Tell them never to sleep in that thatched shed; it's been haunted for years.'

Haunted or not, I would never try to sleep there again, despite the fact that last 15 June several of my friends spent the night inside cooking steaks and drinking coffee while they waited for the dawn.

I would find it hard to choose between the upper and the lower lakes because there is an atmosphere about them both that I cannot explain. I once, at the lower lake, saw what appeared to be a horse and, thinking that it had escaped from the paddock, I approached it. Perhaps it was a trick of the moon, or my imagination, but what appeared to be a substantial animal slowly disappeared. Imagination, no doubt. But some time later the 'lady of the big house' told me that the ghost of a certain horseman often rode around the lakes.

The big house had its ghost, too, she told me, but it was a friendly ghost and it had never caused her a moment's anxiety.

If someone asked me whether or not I believed in ghosts, I think I'd have to hedge a little. I don't really know if I do or not, but I cannot find any logical explanation to what happened to my brother Ken and my cousin Joe at Wadhurst Lake in 1954.

Those two stalwarts decided they would like to fish from the island and so Derrick Davenport and I rowed them across. They pitched their tent among the deep ferns and cut a clearing to the water's edge. They used the cut ferns for bedding and settled down for the night.

Behind the tent was a vast area of 'jungle', mostly fern but with some bramble. In the early hours of the morning they heard what seemed to be an enormous animal approaching the tent. The footsteps were slow and they could hear the undergrowth being crushed as whatever it was drew nearer the tent.

Both said they were petrified as they waited for the tent to be flattened, but then the footsteps stopped and the creature responsible turned and retreated whence it had come. Had there been a boat available, both swore, they would have vacated. As it was they, moved to the water's edge and waited for the dawn.

The odd thing about the whole episode is that there were no traces or prints in the undergrowth next day and no sign whatsoever of any disturbance among the growing plants. The island, as I remember it, was not large and it could hardly have accommodated a deer—which seems the likeliest possibility—which anyway would surely have left some tracks.

How are such things explained? There was no suggestion of a joke involved. We three are closely related and close to each other, and I know that they did not imagine it all.

I am aware that the darkness can play tricks. I know only too well that the familiar tree of the daylight can take on a frightening appearance at night. I know that the rustlings of a vole, the padding of a fox, and the snorts of a badger are magnified at night.

I once had a badger put his head inside my tent at night when I was fishing for carp at Woldale. And here's an odd fact. I had with me my then eleven-year-old daughter, who wanted to fish the night through with me. I would *not* have fished there alone, but with my young daughter present I was relaxed and content. Why should I *not* be scared (I would have been if on my own) simply because I was not alone? I could hardly have relied upon her for protection. Logically, the inquisitive snortings of a badger in the tent ought to have scared me. As it was I felt only deep regret that Valerie did not see it: she was fast asleep in my sleeping bag.

I can remember only one other complete mystery associated with night fishing. It concerns what I have to refer to as a UFO. Joe and I were returning home from a short night stint at a gravel pit in Leighton Buzzard. We had fished until one-thirty in the morning and were cycling home when we saw what we have since referred to as a 'railway carriage in the sky'. It made no sound, and appeared to have lit-up, porthole windows. It was difficult to see whether it was moving or not, but we stopped and looked at it for a full minute or perhaps a little longer. Gradually it pulled away and finally disappeared into the darkness.

There is no doubt that we both saw the same object and we have many times tried to explain it away as a low-flying aircraft. But why no engine sound?

Unlike superstition, these things cannot be put down to coincidence, but there is surely an explanation somewhere. Isn't there?

Night-Glow

I went to visit an old friend some time ago. We had not met since we said goodbye in October '78, and I felt it was time we had another lying session over a bottle of something or other.

It was dark when I arrived, and after a leisurely drink, he insisted that I go down the garden to look over his new 'tackle and gun' room. It had been built with security in mind out of brick and tile. The door was metal-covered and would have served to make Fort Knox itself impregnable. I was impressed and began to consider ways of making my own tackle-den secure. At the time most of my gear, apart from my rifle and my game gun, was somewhere between West Australia and the UK, and kind friends had lent me fly rods and reels.

I should be extra careful with the fly rods since they were not mine, I thought to myself, but I also felt the need for something better than a chain and padlock for my guns; I would eventually have to devise a secure and permanent place for them, and I could do worse than build a structure similar to that of my friend.

'If you do make such a place,' he advised, 'make sure you incorporate a bottle rack. These brick outbuildings make good wine cellars and I've slipped up badly by not thinking about one myself.'

Since I am not a great wine lover I doubt if I shall even consider it, but time will tell.

Crossing the lawn on the way back to the house, I saw what I could only believe to be a remarkably bright glow-worm, and not having seen such a creature for something like twenty years, I hastened to pick it up. It turned out to be a beta-light—one of those remarkable little radio-active tubes that glow in the dark and remain active for many years without the need for recharging. They are, by the way, perfectly safe. You would have to break the tube and swallow the contents before any injury could result.

My friend was pleased. 'I lost that a couple of weeks ago,' he said. 'Searched high and low for it in the daytime and never thought to wait until it was dark to look for it!'

It's something I knew all about myself because I had had more experience with beta-lights than my friend. I once glued one to a float top, fished all night for several nights and congratulated myself on finding a glue that was waterproof and which would really hold. What I had overlooked, however, was the fact that my float top had been stuck *out* of the water while I fished, and for most of the time it had remained reasonably dry.

I left the made-up rod outside while I slept for several hours during the day and, later, when I went to prepare for the next night session, I discovered that the beta-light tip was no longer on the float. It had rained heavily during the day, the glue had dissolved and the tip had fallen into the long grass outside the caravan. I could not find it and so I fished without it. Returning in the pitch darkness of the next early morning, I saw it glowing in the darkness and retrieved it.

There was also a time when I fished a tidal stretch of a little spate river at its height. The water was dirty and I wondered if a lure incorporating a beta-light would show up better in the murk. I taped one to my spinner, cast and became snagged at once. I had to pull for a break and leave both the lure and the beta-light behind. It was then about five in the afternoon. Low tide was six hours later and when I returned in the darkness there was my lure, hanging on to a broken branch and swaying in the breeze.

I was disappointed that what I found on my friend's lawn had not turned out to be a glow-worm, and I cannot help wondering if these creatures still exist in as many spots as they did years ago. Certainly they seem to have disappeared from one of the few places I used to see them—Wotton Lakes. During our summer walks from the upper to the lower lake we used, literally, to follow a trail lit up by glow-worms. They kept to both sides of the narrow path and shone brightly in the long grass.

We often considered enclosing one or two in a transparent float top as Izaak Walton (or someone else) was reputed to have done. We had no luminous tape or paint in those days, and we were looking for some kind of visible aid to our night fishing. Deep down, of course, and in spite of what we'd read about glow-worms, we knew the idea wouldn't work.

I once took a naturalist, who was anxious to acquire some glow-worms, to that very spot. He gathered a harvest of both male and female (he reckoned the females shone more brightly than the males) to plant somewhere in Sussex, and promised to let me know how successful the transfer had been at a later date. He never did, though. Letters travelled back and forth, and enthusiasm reigned until the deed was accomplished. Then silence.

I took half a dozen of those glow-worms home myself, thinking that they would prove interesting to my young daughter. The naturalist told me that they needed snails nearby (or was it slugs?) to survive, and as I had a rock garden full of both, I thought I would establish my own backyard colony. For several nights the glow-worms winked at us as we looked out of the back window. Then I mowed the lawn and remembered too late what I'd done!

I have not seen any glow-worms since those early days. I have vague recollections of soft, striped bodies showing in the light of the torch, but that is all. I am puzzled as to why they have disappeared from their happy hunting grounds, however, since I know for certain that no toxic sprays have ever been used along the banks of the lakes in question. Nor has the ground been tilled or disturbed.

When I was a young man and my long-netting excursions took me to different parts of Buckinghamshire, I sometimes saw glow-worms in the long grass on the edge of a spinney or copse. They could never have been regarded as common—even in those days they were a talking point.

I know nothing much about them, but would I be right, I wonder, in thinking that they did *not* glow every night? It seemed then that there were nights when they were 'out' and others when they were 'in'.

Mention of luminous lures reminds me that on two occasions I have made my bait luminous with immediate success, once when bream fishing in Buckinghamshire, and the other time sea trout fishing in Cumberland. Both times I was worm-fishing and out of curiosity as much as anything else I put two thin strips of luminous tape on my hook before baiting it.

Each time, after a biteless period, I began to catch fish. I recall the sea trout fishing occasion vividly because I had fished for long enough to be desperate. Then I had three fish in quick succession.

Was it coincidence? Would I have had those fish without the luminous material? Of course I'll never know, but since those days

I have toyed with the idea of incorporating a low-powered beta-light in the dressing of a sea trout fly. I think it *might* work, but like a lot more of my ideas it has never been put to the test. I doubt if it ever will.

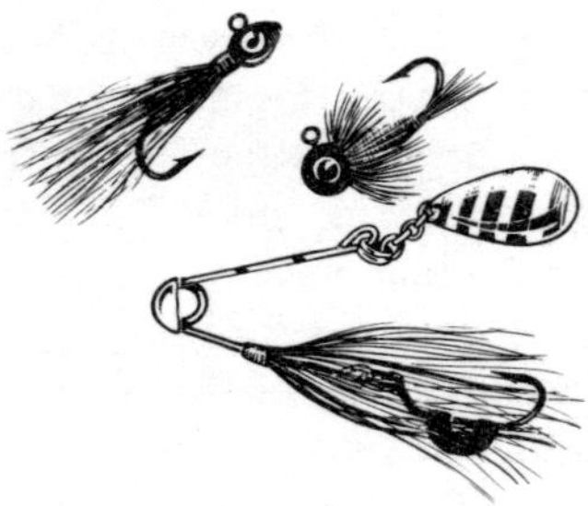

The Frog-Hunters

Many years ago I had a freshly dug pond with no fish in it, but seeing several frogs around it my daughter, then very young, encouraged me to let them stay.

'Please, please,' she wheedled, 'let's have some frog spawn and tadpoles.' And like a fool I agreed.

The pond became a solid mass of jelly and the following year I had to empty it and remove about two hundred frogs. That in itself, was no easy chore, but the real problem lay in disposing of them.

I put them into a big dustbin and let them slop around in an inch or two of water until I'd caught them all. Then I put them into a wet sack and hauled them across the field at the back to a natural farm pond where I released them. 'Good riddance,' said I, very pleased with myself. And I swear, hand on heart, that they were *all* back next day! It took another day's wallowing around in waders to recapture them, and I then dumped them eighteen miles away at the edge of a small lake. Since then I've been fairly free of them, but only after carefully watching for signs of spawn each spring and ruthlessly removing it. This year they sneaked up on me. The fish had a ball, it's true, but they didn't get them all, and if I'm not careful I'll have a sago pudding pond again next year.

Odd creatures, frogs. Likeable, really, I suppose. I once hooked an enormous chub on a big dead frog, and lots of my American friends use them live for bass baits. I've seen then used here for pike but I've never had any desire to engage in such practices myself. I know very little about them, but I've no doubt they fit into nature's general scheme somehow.

A few years ago, when Tring reservoirs were low and the middle banks exposed, it was difficult to move without treading on the thousands of small frogs present. I could see eight herons hunting them down, and I tried hard to figure out what the survival rate could be against such odds.

It is sheer coincidence, I suppose, that a recent message tape from my good friend Bill Hughes in Arkansas reported that the local frog population over there has virtually disappeared. He blames the use of insecticides, just as we did for the apparent decline in our own population over here. But Bill, of course, was referring to the edible frog, and Bill is a frog hunter.

The tales I could tell about Bill and his frogs would make a man's hair curl; but it's a way of life out there, and frog-hunting is a legitimate sport. There is a season on frogs and a bag limit is imposed. Penalties for contravention are severe.

We were camped once, in northern Illinois, on opening day, and Bill asked me if I fancied trying my hand at 'gigging'. I declined because I was tired and, as the thought of a midnight wallow in the swamp didn't appeal to me very much, I went to sleep.

I was awakened in the early hours by what I can only describe as a ghastly sight. Bill, clad only in underpants, legs plastered in black smelly mud, had a great bull frog impaled on the end of a three-pronged spear which he held inches from my face. In the light of the lamp on his forehead it was a gruesome sight and I, having been awakened from a deep sleep, couldn't see the funny side of it. In today's parlance it might be referred to as a 'traumatic experience'. Traumatic or not, however, frogs' legs *are* good to eat. And the American hunters' ways *are* effective if not entirely pleasant.

There are many ways of catching frogs over there, just as there are many ways of catching rabbits over here. And, as my American friends view ferreting with horror, I try to keep an open mind.

Whoever heard of hunting frogs with a spinning rod? It's true, however. Only a meat-hunter like Bill Hughes could have dreamed it up, but it works. It requires a deal of skill, as do all methods of hunting, but it is practical, selective and exciting.

Small surface popping plugs are used, and the object is to tease the frogs into attacking. I'm told that these frogs are short-sighted and I'm prepared to believe it in view of what happens. There, on the bank, sits a big bull frog caring about nothing much in particular, when, in front of it, six inches from its nose, a small object plops into the water and begins to gurgle along the surface. It sits up and takes notice then, and several casts later, able to stand this intruder upon its silence no longer, the frog leaps and nails it. And whether or not it is short-sighted, it does manage to hit the intruder open-mouthed.

For a few seconds it's a case of all-get-out, then, eventually, it is hauled ashore and either dispatched or put into the 'live box'. Only an Arkansas Hillbilly could behave in such outrageous fashion and, as Bill reckons he has one leg shorter than the other through working the Ozark Hills, I suppose the cap fits. It *is* fun though.

A long way north, in Minnesota, the resident fishermen used to fish at night with frog baits when the walleye were working the shorelines. It was the generally accepted custom until their frog population, too, disappeared. That kind of fishing is no longer commonplace and methods have changed a little. But so, too, have the fishing methods of the blue herons. At one time they waded and picked up frogs. Now they land on water up to a hundred feet deep, and float with outspread wings, waiting for their food to come to them. Getting airborne again from such an attitude ought to be impossible, but somehow they manage to achieve what is literally a vertical lift-off. Had I not seen it for myself I would not have believed it.

It took but two years for these herons to adapt to these conditions and their ability to do so serves as a prime example of survival technique. I've no idea how widespread the practice has become, but I have seen if often enough in the lake areas where I have fished to convince me that it is fairly commonplace. I have, in fact found myself wondering whether bluegills—the commonest fish in the Minnesota lake complex—which tend to seek the shelter of, for instance, weedbeds, are drawn by the shade provided by the herons' wings. If this is, in fact, the case, I can only marvel at the sheer efficiency involved.

Years ago, a big frog population in one of my ponds attracted several grass-snakes. Only Mother Nature knows how such things come about, but I considered it highly unusual at the time. After all, grass-snakes could hardly be regarded as creatures likely to be found in semi-built-up areas.

But the scheme of things is such that bumper harvests have to be reaped and compensations have to be made for shortages. It works throughout the whole of the countryside, and even the humble frog seemingly plays its part.

The Irish Minnesotan

In a lifetime's involvement with what might be generally referred to as outdoor sports, I have made a lot of friends. It was always easy to do because of the common bond that exists between those who share the same interests, ideals and passions.

'Birds of a feather ...' they say, and it is true that, in all walks of life, people who have common interests invariably seek out and find each other. But, in the case of field sports, there's a little more to it. It is not necessary to be a wildfowler to appreciate the fowler's point of view; not necessary to be an angler to understand what makes an angler tick. I've never shot a deer in my life, and have no desire to do so, but one of my best friends hunts them with a bow and arrow. I've never hunted coon, but I recognise the love, dedication and enthusiasm that exists between my American coon-hunting friends and the hounds they train to perfection. I understand their pride although I do not understand the finer points of their sport.

I have hunting friends who have never held a fishing rod and who are half-scared of ferrets, but whose friendship I value because they accept that I am a hunter too, though of a different kind.

I would be hard put to single out any one friend for special mention, but the more I think of Cecil Porter, the more I believe him to be a complete story in his own right.

Cecil (or Ceese as he is commonly called) is a third-generation Irish Minnesotan. He speaks with a brogue that is as Irish as peat and porter, but, being the husband (and despair) of a charming Norwegian lady called Gunda, he occasionally gets his accents a little mixed. He was seventy years young when I first met him; he is now well into his eighties and going strong. He is a hunter, fisher, poacher, berry-picker, wine-maker and general harvester of the good things nature provides each year.

I first fished with Cecil through the ice on a Minnesota lake many years ago. It was twenty degrees or so below zero outside, though in his little insulated fish house the evil-smelling oil stove belched smoke and heat that had had us stripped to shirt-sleeve order in double-quick time.

The dividing line between death by freezing and death by asphyxiation was exceedingly narrow, I thought, but Cecil put a cud of snoose (some kind of vile chewing snuff) under his bottom lip and fished unconcernedly. 'Whoy don't dey boit, Fred?' he'd ask every so often. 'Goddammit, Oim yigging goot.'

We caught tullibees that day and for several days after we ate them smoked. Cecil was well over seventy-five then and never missed a day's fishing for as long as the ice would bear. He's a great fisher.

He is also a deer hunter—albeit a little different from most. Having his own farmland, Cecil believes in hunting deer in *his* way and at what *he* considers to be the right time. Seasons and limits never bothered Cecil too much.

He was, and still is, a great and sincere conservationist and would never over-exploit a harvest, but some of his minor escapades gave cause for suspicion among the game wardens.

Cecil gave them food for more suspicion by walking into the local restaurant where they took their midday break and announcing gaily that he'd killed 'a foine big buck yesterday' or that he'd had 'two more last week'. After a time the wardens cottoned on and eventually began to ask, 'How many this week, then, Cecil?' And Cecil would dream up a figure just to keep them happy. They, in turn, would grin, give knowing winks to all present and leave. Cecil, they thought, was quite harmless.

'How many today then?' asked the warden one day in November.

'Only one,' answered Cecil. 'A big buck. It's over there in the pick-up truck.'

The warden laughed and moved on. Cecil climbed back into the pick-up truck, breathed a sigh of relief, and drove off with a twelve-pointer hidden beneath the tarpaulin cover.

He hunted foxes, too, until a few years ago. His hunts were a little different from those we know over here but they provided beyond any shadow of doubt a real and exciting chase. Cecil and his followers would meet at sun-up and chase the fox across the frozen wastes of the Minnesota lake system. They used no hounds and their mounts were snowmobiles.

'Sometimes we'd run one down,' Cecil told me, 'but mostly dey'd git away. Dey give us a helluva run and dat was real fun. You bat.'

Having 'ridden shotgun' on the back of Cecil's snowmobile many times, and having had difficulty in both breathing and staying on, I believe that 'helluva good run' part!

He had, until 1978, never caught carp on rod and line and, knowing me to be interested in carp, he sorted out a spot on the Red River that borders Minnesota and North Dakota.

Cecil wanted to catch a carp too.

'Oi've speared the sons-o'-bitches,' he said, 'but niver caught one reg'lar.'

'You will today, Cecil,' I said. I could see huge sheets of bubbles and it was obvious that carp were present and feeding. The North Dakota bank looked the better of the two but, having only Minnesota licences, we stayed on our own side of the bridge.

Cecil, a great believer in tackle strong enough to hold a horse, had difficulty in casting and in recognising bites until I took away his unsuitable gear and gave him one of my own light carp outfits.

The first cast he executed sailed well past the halfway mark and he chuckled. 'Don't need two licences now,' he said. 'Dammit, Oi can fish in Dakotee any time Oi loike.'

Jack Vasconcellos, the other member of our party, and I caught several carp while Cecil remained fishless, and the stringer was almost full when he finally hit into a carp that literally scared him.

'Here, Yack,' he said. 'You foight de son-of-a-bitch.' Jack quietly told him to fight his own fish: 'You hooked it—you take care of it.' And Cecil, with encouragement from both of us, did just that.

It was by far the biggest carp of the day and Cecil gloated. He had arranged to have the fish smoked by another friend and, with about a round dozen on the stringer, he was about to go back in a blaze of glory.

Disaster struck when I tried to add yet another carp to the total. Cecil's big fish slipped the stringer and escaped into the depths of the river. It had to be the biggest fish, of course. Odd's law accounts for that.

I apologised profusely. 'I feel real bad about it, Cecil,' I said.

Cecil snarled, 'Be Jasus not half as bad as I do.' And for the rest of the week he told of how Jack and I had released his fish because he'd caught one bigger than ours.

The carp were duly smoked, sampled and pronounced delicious.

The night before I left, I sat in Cecil's home, drank of the wine he had made from local wild grapes, and ate of Gunda's home-made cookies.

As I kissed Gunda's cheek in farewell salute, Cecil, mean as ever, remarked that this goddam limey not only steals his fish but tries to steal his wife as well—be Jasus!

But his grip was firm, his goodbye was, I thought, as reluctant as was mine, and his invitation to return was sincere. 'Damn you, you come back, d'ye hear?' he commanded.

And if time and the Good Lord allow it, Cecil, I promise that I will. You bat.

The Versatile Bluegill

As I have said before, I could not begin to count the number of times I have been asked to nominate my favourite fish, nor the number of times I have given the stock reply, 'It's the one I'm fishing for at the time.' That, to many, might be regarded as a cop-out, and of course it is. But there's also a great deal of truth involved. There are certain species for which I no longer fish because they hold no further interest for me. They would never make my shortlist of favourite species, and so they could never be considered to be in the running. Of the remainder, some give me pleasure because they're difficult, others (because I've put in time and learned a little of their habits) please me because they can be tracked down by logic. Others offer unusual sporting or fighting qualities, and so on. Each situation is different; each holds a certain pleasure the others may not have and, for that reason alone, I will not be compromised into naming a favourite British fish.

But give me more scope—include the freshwater fish of the great American continent, and I will, without hesitation, make my choice. The very humble, eager, scrappy, delicious, prolific, and beautiful bluegill. Nowhere in this world have I found a fish with so many qualities, so much get-up-and-go, or so much response to so many fishing methods.

What other species will take wet or dry fly, spoon, spinner, jig, plug, live or dead minnow, plastic worm, sweetcorn, surface popper or worm? (I could go on for much longer if necessary for I doubt if there's any end to what a bluegill will take.)

What other fish, I wonder, can fight so hard for its size that one famous outdoor writer says of it with great conviction, 'If they all weighed six pounds we'd still be wondering what they looked like'?

Those are my favourite fish—the ones I never tire of catching, because of the great variety of method, location, presentation and technique involved. I am not normally a jealous person, but I envy the Americans their bluegills and I wish we had them in Britain. Any mention of importing alien fish, however, brings about emotional outcries from those who appear to be against any form of conservation experiment. Many of those who object regularly catch limits of rainbow trout from stocked waters and give no thought to the fact that a hundred years ago *those* were very much alien fish.

As I write this, I can see the bluegills rising from the boat dock in the lake thirty yards from where I sit. There's a fly rod leaning against the cottonwood tree, and an English match rod resting lengthwise along the aluminium boat. In the garage is a made-up ultra-light spinning rod and a reel loaded with 3-pound test line and I know that, at any time, I could pick up one or other of those rods and catch a bluegill.

It wouldn't be big, in fact it would be very small for the lake in question. I would have to take out the boat and look for cover before I found the big ones. And by big I simply mean fish weighing perhaps a little less than a pound. I've had them bigger. Once, by sheer luck, I had a near two-pounder, but those less than half that weight are the table-sized fish—the size you can fillet.

Jack Vasconcellos, my host and guide, is a superb bluegill fisherman. He has a favourite saying about size limits. 'If they don't fillet, they don't stay.' (Americans don't fillet fish—they 'fillày' them, and Jack's self-imposed size limit comes across in rhyme.)

I have caught my share and eaten my fill of them this time. Their meat is sweet and firm, and I truly prefer them to some Atlantic salmon I have eaten. And later today I will catch some more—if I fish at all, that is.

I may have to return ten undersized fish for every keeper, or I may hit gold and catch thirty (the legal limit) keepers in succession.

I may catch them on a fly rod and a small streamer fly, I may jig for them down in twelve feet of water, or I may put up my float tackle and catch them on corn. It makes little difference to me. I enjoy all methods and because, out here, I am unfettered by restrictions, I can change as the mood takes me. I *don't want* to be casting a fly all day, any more than I want to spin or bait-fish. I like to be free to make my choice, to exploit and explore the depths, to experiment, to catch fish, and be pleased when my ploys work. Restrict my numbers of fish by all means, but do not hamstring me and frustrate me by making me use a method I know to be useless in certain circumstances.

I refuse to flog away with fly tackle on an English reservoir when I know full well I could enjoy better fishing if I were allowed to present that self-same fly on a different outfit. Out here I am encouraged to fish; allowed to take my limit of several species in the same day if I'm smart enough and feel inclined to do so. And no one is more pleased to see me do it than the local anglers and conservationists.

Catching these hard-fighting little fish requires little technical ability, but undoubtedly the rate of catching can be speeded up by using fly or jig tackle. That way no time is lost in baiting up. The artificial lure will possibly catch two more fish during the time it takes to rebait a hook. But there are times when bait catches the deeper-lying, better-quality fish. The problem then lies in getting through the layers of smaller fish above them. Most times it's impossible, but every so often, with a heavy shot placed very close to the hook, the bait makes it down to the right depth. Then it is usually only a matter of seconds before the float disappears and the rod tip bends towards the water.

You think a rainbow fights, a sea trout has power, a tench bores, a pike leaps, a salmon strips line from the spool, a barbel hangs heavy in the current? Scale them all down to the same weight of one pound, put them in their own environment, and I swear that none of them could perform like the humble bluegill, hooked on fine tackle down at the twelve-foot level in these limpid Minnesota lakes.

Yesterday, in search of better fish, I put on one of my big black-and-white streamer flies. I fished it loaded with swanshot and cast it with a light, soft-actioned spinning rod and 3-pound line. It wasn't a 'catch-lots-of-fish' operation, but rather a 'let's-see-if-we-can-get-a-big-one' venture.

The black-and-white streamer, the Integration (looks more like a 'minner' than a 'minner'), was tied to a No. 2 hook and I fished it back over the weed tops at around six feet. It really isn't meant for bluegills, but they socked it good and hard several times at long range and fought every inch of the way back to the boat.

There is no end to bluegill fishing. Nor is there any beginning. No special time of day or season. Bluegills almost invariably bite. They appeat to be permanently hungry while remaining as fat as tiny piglets.

In the spring the aggressive males will hit anything that lands near them on the surface and at anything passing them by below it. Their bright blue gill-covers and their orange throats and breasts shimmer in the sunlight and their great spiny dorsals rise in anger to spike the unwary angler. They will never attain the dignity of the carp or the majesty of the salmon but they are characters in their own right.

When the temperature has been in the region of 90°F, I have waded barefoot but fully clothed into the lake's warm water and teased bluegills out of the weedbeds with reservoir-trout tackle.

I have also put on a snowmobile suit and snowshoes, hauled a loaded sledge across the lake and fished through forty inches of ice to catch bluegills with the air temperature at 15°F below zero or lower.

That is what I call versatility. No close season, no restriction and still no shortage. In fact, it would appear from all accounts that the harder bluegills are fished, the better the fishing becomes. What angler could ask for more?

I have caught bluegills almost clear across the USA from the brackish rivers of Florida and the muddy ponds of Illinois, to the rippling, white-diamond-spangled waters of Michigan and Minnesota, and I've never tired of them.

Perhaps it's because the good advice given to me by my American friends, added to my own fishing experiences in Britain, makes their capture fairly easy. Perhaps I'm now ready to quit the struggle for bigger and better fish and enjoy something easier and less demanding. On the other hand, I first fished bluegills in this very spot exactly ten years ago and I loved them then just as much as I do today.

A Day with Largemouth

With an official estimate of 10.4 million acres of land under water in seven states of America, Jack Erhesman and I gave up the idea of trying to fish in any of the big impoundments and chose instead to fish some of the local strip-mines.

It was a wise choice. Instead of thick soup we found crystal-clear water and luxurious weed growth. We also found some fish! True, they were not big fish, but at least they were eager biters and our brief stay was enhanced by the fact that we were getting a fish every cast at one stage.

I've caught many largemouth bass up to six pounds during my several visits to this country but I cannot recall a time when I caught so many in so short a period. I found it especially interesting, too, because, although it was strictly lure and jig fishing, we were able to fish the whole time from the bank.

When the water begins to warm up, largemouth bass begin to work the shoreline for food and it is the general practice, on big waters at any rate, to fish from a boat. The cast is made then so as to place the lure an inch or two from the bank and retrieve it through the deeper water towards the boat. It works well enough, and thousands of bass are caught that way each year. It's a method I've practised a lot in England too, for pike especially, and I've found it useful when the banks have been overgrown and the waterline difficult to reach from land. But I am sure that there are times when boat noises, particularly the rattling of oars on a wooden punt, do much to scare the fish away. And I believe that many fish here are also scared away by approaching boats, especially those with powerful engines.

Leon Zedric, the fisheries manager on the strip-mines we visited, put forward an interesting theory—one with which I agreed entirely. Bass, he said, often lie in wait several yards from the shoreline and drive their prey towards the banks where they can corner it in the shallow water, and a lure fished towards the bank instead of away from it probably appears more acceptable at certain times of the year.

We found it so. Nearly all the bass we caught were hooked

close to the bank on which we stood, but there was strong evidence to suggest that our lures had been followed by fish lying out in the deeper water. I've no idea what the biggest fish we caught would have weighed but I doubt if any went more than twelve ounces, and I've no idea how many we caught as I stopped counting after we'd unhooked and released about fifty.

But it was interesting and stimulating, to say the least. We were using ultra-light rods, tiny jig-spinners and lines of about 3-pound test. The little fish fought every inch of the way and often forced us to give line, so powerful were their outward runs against the tiny wands we were using. Later I changed to fly and had some real fun with these scrappy little fish.

There would have been no enjoyment in it at all had we been using regular bass tackle, but on our light outfits those fish were real fun to catch. I doubt very much if we could have handled any of the five-, six- and seven-pounders known to inhabit the lake we were fishing, but it would have been interesting to have had the opportunity.

No big fish came our way, however, but proof of their existence was there in the shape of three super bass that Leon had caught the day previously. They were alive and well in a big wire cage, and I admired and photographed them before Leon went to work on them with the big fillet knife.

'Stay to supper,' he invited. 'We'll have bass fillets and fresh-picked mushrooms.' And he showed me a huge boxful of morrells he had gathered that morning. They were sponge-like fungi, and although I have never eaten them I imagine that Leon's proposed meal would have been a gourmet's delight. But I had a bus to catch that evening and I declined, reluctantly.

'Before you go,' said Leon, 'you must catch some of our red-eared sunfish. They're like bluegills and I know you'll enjoy them.' He knew, by now, that bluegills are my favourite American fish and he knew of a spot where they lay in abundance.

So with our little jig rods we followed Leon along the dusty trail (amazing after all that rain), coughing and spluttering in his wake. The sunfish were there, eager, scrappy little fish weighing less than a pound but strong and beautiful as their many-coloured bodies flashed brilliantly in the gin-clear water.

How different this was from flogging away in the murk of the big lakes we had visited previously, and how good it was to see the shapes of fish swimming deep among the dark green weed-beds again.

I would never have tired of it, I'm sure, but time was pressing and I reluctantly had to consider packing my rods away and getting back to the city.

Jack and I looked for Leon, but he had disappeared and, in that vast expanse of land and water, there was no way we could find him. Nor was there any way for us to get out. Leon had locked the gates behind us and we were stranded. We were still stranded long after the bus I ought to have caught had left!

Then, over the brow of the hill came Leon. Rod in hand, hat pushed back, he staggered under the weight of a bulky haversack. As he came to a halt he remarked, 'I thought you might like to take back a mixed bag, Fred, so I brung you some crappie.' And from the big haversack he tossed one, two, three, eight, fine black crappie. 'Now,' he said, 'get busy with your fillet knife.' I hadn't the heart to tell him I'd missed my bus, but in a way I was glad.

Later that evening at Jack's house I teamed up with three fine young boys—fishermen in the making. Jack's son Doug, Scott and Gary Matteson and I joined forces to catch bluegills from the small lake at the bottom of Jack's garden, while he worked over the outdoor stove frying smelt, crappie and bluegills for us to eat there and then.

Why is it, I wonder, that small fish cooked and eaten out of doors taste so good? They're delicious at any time, of course, but that fresh-air flavour just has to be experienced to be appreciated.

It's part of the whole American fishing scene and I never tire of it.

I wish we in England had fish like bass and bluegills. I wish we had the climate to encourage us to do similar things. I wish we had vast waters to fish, and fish that were as easy for our youngsters to catch as those which are accepted naturally as part of the American way of life. I wish—but I could go on wishing . . . .

Momma's Bait

The sign off Highway 36, Illinois, read: 'Carp fishing 2 dollars per day', and Charlie Bowen pulled on to the farm track and followed the signs to the lake. It was a small commercial 'pay lake'—only three or four acres in extent which had been built, filled and stocked the previous spring. The owner, Harry Emrick, told us that 3,600 pounds of Wisconsin carp had been introduced, some two hundred of which weighed over twenty pounds. Times of fishing were from eight in the morning until eight in the evening, but Harry seemed to like my English accent and told me I could fish all night if I wished. So I did!

Charlie Bowen and I arrived after the last daytime angler had left and, as we were setting up our tackle, we were joined by Harry and his partner, who had decided to try their luck at night too.

I had my Mark IV carp rod, Charlie had his also, but Harry and his friend put up little, short, stumpy, solid glass affairs with which they fished tight-line style. I was quite sure that they were not going to catch anything because, as everyone knows, you just *don't* catch carp on tight lines.

I stuck with soft bread-paste and crust bait. Harry had a sweet, yellow concoction which reeked of aniseed and which he called 'Momma's bait'. His mother, he told me, made it by the batch, kept it refrigerated, and sold it at the bait–tackle–cold drinks kiosk which she ran on the lakeside during the day.

It was indeed a privilege to be allowed to night-fish at this very well-stocked lake, I thought, as I cast into the deep water near the dam end.

Suddenly the whole lake became flood-lit and Harry said that just because it was night there was no need to fool around in complete darkness! (I later learned that it was his policy to keep the lake floodlit at night to discourage poachers.) I groaned with dismay and there and then wrote off any chance of catching a carp, but I refrained from voicing my feelings.

How little I knew about American carp and American carp-fishing methods! It didn't matter that the lake was floodlit, it didn't matter that Harry and his friend simply did not seem to know the need for quiet.

It didn't matter that they were using rods totally unsuited to carp fishing, that their hooks were crude and much too large, or that their tight-line methods would be sure to result in lost fish in England.

Those carp didn't know the rules! They didn't know that bread-paste and crust were far better carp baits than sweet and scented concoctions. They didn't know that you can't set a big hook with a tooth-pick rod or that they were supposed to reject the bait the the moment they felt the rod tip's resistance. In fact those carp didn't play fair at all! They took Harry's aniseed baits and nearly pulled his rods in each time they took. My delicately set Mark IV outfits remained solidly in their rod rests, bale arms open, luminous dolly indicators perfectly still.

I was sure that Harry knew the hotspot and that there were no carp in my chosen swim, but he assured me that my bait was at fault. If only I would use Momma's bait, he assured me, I would begin to catch carp and, after Harry and his friend had caught nine and I none, I allowed myself to be persuaded. It was a good job that I did. Throughout that night I fished bread on one rod and Momma's bait on the other and, although only a few feet separated the baits, I had no bites at all on the bread.

Of course things could have been different. The fish we caught ranged only between three and four pounds apiece and all of them were enthusiastic about biting. Had the lake been in complete darkness, the big fish might have fed. Had they done so they might have chosen to eat simple bread baits and, it is possible, I suppose, that my orthodox carp tackle might have been a better proposition for the big fellows. I tried to convince myself of this but, if the truth be told, I didn't really succeed in doing so!

We caught, in all, thirty-three common carp and, although we did not catch any truly worthwhile fish, I have to admit that I cannot remember ever having so many carp bites in a single night. Nor do I remember a night (or even a week) when my big landing net was put to use so many times.

In The Wilderness

It is four hundred or more miles from Minneapolis to Jellicoe, Canada, and taking turns to drive we covered it in one long haul. There were nine of us with rods, tackle, baits, provisions, sleeping bags, cameras and clothing in two vehicles, one of which was a mini-bus; and our journey was non-stop apart from stops for petrol and customs clearance at Pigeon River.

Base camp at Cedar Springs, Jellicoe, North Ontario, was the end of the road and only logging trails continued further north. We stayed there overnight after purchasing the essential licences, mosquito coils and fly dope, and the following morning we loaded our incredible pile of gear on to one of the small float-planes in readiness for the fly-in shuttle.

It took three trips before we were all installed in the wilderness camp at Ogoki Lake. Each trip took almost an hour, during which time we flew over lakes and timber country for a distance of almost a hundred miles. Purely for interest's sake I counted over seventy lakes on my side of the plane during one full minute's flying! It is impossible to describe the vastness of that great country, but these facts may convey some small idea of it.

After organising ourselves and settling into the primitive but adequate camp, all our thoughts were centred on fishing and on catching enough fish for our supper that night.

There were four boats moored by the jetty and an Indian guide, resident in the nearby bush, kept their motors serviceable. He knew the water well, of course, and when we were ready to start fishing he took Bill Hughes and me to a spot some five miles away to spin for pike and walleye. We caught only small pike during that brief period between then and lunch time, and since I do not have to travel to a Canadian wilderness camp to catch pike, but can catch all I need in Britain, I proposed that the afternoon should be spent jigging for walleye.

A big red plastic bottle had been anchored in the walleye hot-spot, and for most of the afternoon we busied ourselves catching two-pounders for supper.

We were reasonably selective and returned all small fish but, although the fishing was fair, it was not exceptionally brisk. We returned that evening with enough fish to feed the whole camp and, while the two volunteer cooks prepared supper, I helped to fillet and pack the remainder in ice. There still remained scores of huge ice blocks in the big underground bunker despite the July heat. These blocks are cut from the lake in November each year and are stored under their covering of sawdust until the next ice forms.

Dan Gapen, lure manufacturer, angler extraordinary, and son of Don Gapen, the inventor of the famous Muddler Minnow fly, was our host and he chose to team up with me for two days. We encountered some remarkable walleye spots and hauled out literally hundreds of fish, some of which were in the five-to-six-pound range. We tried to beat each other in competition, played dirty tricks to prevent the other from scoring, and eventually agreed that we would like something more difficult.

It is odd, is it not, that all anglers dream of a situation where they can catch a good fish at every cast and yet, when such a spot is located, look for something requiring more skill. Most of the fish we caught could have been taken by an absolute novice. It was enjoyable for a time and, had we needed more fish to eat, it would have been ideal, but the novelty of it all quickly faded.

We motored around, hauled our boat through swamps and shallows, tried to find big pike in the weed-beds and caught a number approaching double figures. This was spinning water of the finest quality. It was also clean, cool and drinkable. We had hundreds of square miles of it at our disposal and it would have taken a lifetime to come to terms with one small corner of it all. Nevertheless we felt the urge to explore other aspects, particularly the rocky river that flowed into the main lake.

Dan, a superb boat handler, pushed the craft up into the rapids and, with motor and paddle, somehow found the smoother, higher level.

I doubt if those rapids had ever before been negotiated otherwise than by canoe, and thoughts of the journey back scared me a little. In the meantime, however, we pushed on upstream, stopping here and there to explore deep holes and minor rapids with fly rods. It was not a big-fish exercise, but an expedition up a river where few, if any, white men had ever trod.

There was a remote silence and splendour about it all that defied description. Every yard of water seemed different. Every hole and boulder had a tale to tell and in the midst of it all we knew there were fish to be caught. Walleye and pike, sauger and whitefish, possibly brown and brook trout.

In a fifty-foot-deep hole something nailed my small lure and bored. I bent into it with the tiny five-foot rod, and Dan gave me power from the outboard. The reel clutch slipped, scorching my finger, and forty yards downstream a pike broke the water and tail-walked on the surface. It was a lean, mean fish, streamlined and athletic as all pike should be. There is a tremendous difference between these pike and our own native over-fed specimens that can only come to light in a stand-up fight. It took, perhaps, ten minutes to subdue that fish. An English specimen of the same length would have weighed twenty pounds. This one weighed little more than half of that. It tried to bite the boat paddle in two while I removed the hook, and I returned it to the water by hanging the paddle over the side of the boat. For a time it hung on angrily but, when I lowered it into the water, it let go and disappeared in a shower of spray. I was not impressed with the size of the fish but its power was remarkable.

Here and there, the river divided and small backwaters formed alongside boulder-strewn rapids. The current was powerful and I noted that attractive pools had formed where small waterfalls had scoured the river bed. This was fly water of the best. Trout were almost certainly present but we failed to contact them.

Instead my little jet-black wet fly searched the swirling eddies and accounted for both walleye and sauger. Dan, using one of his father's famous Muddlers, fared equally well. There was little to choose between us.

A sudden pull almost unbalanced me from my position on a smooth rock, something tore upstream against the pull of the current at a speed that amazed me and within seconds the line parted. I was convinced at once that it was either different from or better than anything I had hooked previously, and I made a great deal of speculative capital about it. If only I could have seen it, I wailed, but now we should never know—and so on. We have all said it before so many times.

Five minutes later Dan landed a small pike with my black fly set firmly in its jaw. There has to be a moral there somewhere.

As the day wore on and we explored more and more of that magnificent river, we forgot our friends on the lake ten miles away, and lost all track of time. We had neither food nor drink with us and our only sustenance came from the water which we scooped from the river in an enamel mug.

Perhaps it was my hunger that warned me of approaching night; perhaps it was the thought of negotiating those rapids in the dark that made me suggest we should return to camp. Whatever reason, it was as well we did.

After taking a wrong fork and having to transport boat, motor and tackle across an impenetrable wall of boulders as well as coming perilously near to capsizing in the home stretch rapids, we finally made camp by the light of a log fire lit by the other members of the party. They assured us it had not been lit for our benefit but to barbecue the last of the remaining steaks.

I will not try to describe the meal we ate that night. Even today I can still savour the freshly caught fish and those seared and sizzling chunks of tender beef.

In spite of the sheer light-heartedness of the whole venture, and the fact that I was using prototype tackle and lures for much of the time, I doubt if I have ever caught a bigger weight of fish in any single week before or since.

I may have caught more fish, and there have been times when I have become blasé about big catches, but for sheer poundage I have yet to encounter fishing like that provided by the Ogoki Wilderness. There were no real specimens to start us bragging and most of the pike we caught would have been cursed by the average English pike fisher, but all were caught on rods weighing little more than two ounces and on tiny jigs armed with only single hooks. By specimen standards our five-to-six-pound walleye were nearer the mark, but the methods we used were not aimed at the big deep-lying monsters. We fished only for food and fun.

On the last morning of our stay in camp, two hours' fishing produced nine limits of fish, all of which were filleted, packed in ice and loaded aboard the float-plane when it came to take us out.

I had been bitten half to death by black flies and mosquitoes,

I had been frozen half stiff in an icy electric storm, I had been roasted in the sun, soaked to the skin in the rain and I had been scared. Now I needed clean clothes, a hot bath and the other refinements of civilisation. Despite all that, however, I wanted to stay on in that great wilderness and I would have done so had it been possible, simply to revel in the sheer magnificence of it all for a little longer.

There is indeed more to fishing than catching fish. I knew it before I went there, but the great Ogoki Wilderness reminded me of it yet again.

Cannon-Ball Coho

'I've heard of hand grenades,' I said, 'but cannon-ball fishing I just do not believe!' That was in 1967 when I was first invited to fish for the coho salmon of Lake Michigan with what was then called the 'cannon-ball rig'. Since then I have fished for coho many times and on a recent trip to the United States I fished with the cannon balls once again.

It is a simple but effective rig. The lure on the light sport-fishing outfit is taken down to something like ninety feet by means of a big six- or seven-pound lead ball attached to a separate downrigger wire, and is held to fish at that depth through the coho salmon shoals. When a salmon hits the lure it breaks free from the heavy ball and is played to the surface on the light gear. Then the downrigger, the so-called cannon ball, is wound to the surface and the tackle is re-set.

It is a common practice among the regular boat fishers of

Michigan to arm their cannon balls with an extra lure apart from those on the sporting rigs, and very often this lure will account for a bonus fish. It is strategically placed, *not* for sport but for fish pure and simple. It is, in fact, referred to as the meat hook. Any coho salmon taken on the meat hook can show no fight and is simply cranked to the surface on the heavy wire along with the lead ball and other ironmongery. There is no sport involved nor is it in any way exciting. That is how it had always appeared to me, and the annoying thing was that for some reason the coho seemed to prefer the meat hook to the lure on the sporting rig.

On another visit some years later things seemed to be much the same. The cannon balls were set with the meat hooks in place and sure enough the first fish, a ten-pounder, hit one of them and was hauled aboard with little ceremony and dumped into the cooler box. It was a nice fish which would be good to eat, but no one really enjoyed catching it.

We had a similar hit a few hours later, this time with a few changes. The fish was not a coho but a chinook salmon—a twenty-three-pounder and full of steam.

It snarled itself and the cannon ball to which it was attached around a second rig off the stern of the boat. Then, towing two seven-pound balls and yards and yards of wire, it hurled itself to the surface from ninety feet below. Not content with that, it jumped and jumped and jumped again, shaking its head in fury and bewilderment. Had I not seen it, I could not have believed it. I would not have thought it possible for a fish to drag nearly two-thirds of its own weight up through ninety feet of water and still be capable of acrobatics at the end of it.

When it was finally subdued there was an almighty tangle to sort out and it was over an hour before we could fish again. There never was such a mess aboard a rocking boat.

They told me it often took over an hour to beat a chinook and, having seen this one perform, I can well believe it.